TWAYNE'S WORLD AUTHORS SERIES
A Survey of the World's Literature

SPAIN

Gerald Wade, Vanderbilt University
Janet W. Diáz, University of North Carolina at Chapel Hill

EDITORS

Juan Boscán

TWAS 475

LAS OBRAS

DE BOSCAN Y ALGVNAS DE GAR
CILASSO DELA VEGA REPAR
TIDAS EN QVATRO
LIBROS.

PLVS
VL·TRA.

PLVS
VL·TRA.

CVM PRIVILEGIO
IMPERIALI.

CARLES AMOROS

JUAN BOSCÁN

By DAVID H. DARST
Florida State University

TWAYNE PUBLISHERS
A DIVISION OF G. K. HALL & CO., BOSTON

Library of Congress Cataloging in Publication Data

Darst, David H
Juan Boscán.

(Twayne's world authors series ; TWAS 475 : Spain)

Bibliography: p. 128–32
Includes index.
1. Boscán Almogaver, Juan, d. 1542—Criticism
and interpretation.
PQ6279.B6D3   861'.3   77–22158
ISBN 0–8057–6316–3

For Patricia and Henry

Contents

About the Author

David H. Darst received his collegiate degrees from the University of the South (Sewanee), the University of North Carolina at Chapel Hill, and the University of Kentucky, respectively. Since 1970 he has been teaching in the Department of Modern Languages at Florida State University. His professional credentials include a Fulbright fellowship to Spain, research grants from the National Endowment for the Humanities and the American Philosophical Society, a score of articles on all aspects of Spanish civilization of the Golden Age, and two books: *The Comic Art of Tirso de Molina* (Chapel Hill: Estudios de Hispanófila, 1974) and *Tirso de Molina's 'The Trickster of Seville:' A Critical Commentary* (New York: Monarch Notes, 1976). Professor Darst is on the editorial board of several journals and is book review editor for the *Journal of Hispanic Philology*.

Preface

This book will be the first comprehensive study of the life and works of Juan Boscán since Marcelino Menéndez Pelayo's volume in *Antología de poetas líricos castellanos* at the turn of the present century. This work will also be the first to make the poet and his lyrics available to a non-Hispanic audience. It therefore attempts to present all aspects of Boscán's career and poetic growth, even though many of them will already be familiar to scholars and specialists in sixteenth-century Spanish literature. At the same time, the study tries to show why Boscán wrote the particular kind of poetry that he did, and how he achieved in some of his poems the poetic brilliance that has led to his acclaim by later critics as the father of Spanish Renaissance poetry. The book is therefore both an informative historical survey of the poet's life and artistic development as well as an anthology of stylistic analyses of his most representative pieces.

In accordance with the general format of volumes in the Twayne World Authors Series, this study presents the life and times of the subject in Chapter One, then dedicates the remaining chapters to an examination of his works. The chapter divisions in this particular case were ready-made. Although Boscán died before his poetry was published and the final editing and proofreading were done by his wife, Ana Girón de Rebolledo, he had so nearly concluded the preparations that Ana Girón published the poems as he had left them. The complete volume of his poetry, entitled *The Works of Boscán and Some of Garcilaso de la Vega, Separated into Four Books,* contains three books of the Catalan's lyrics and one book of Garcilaso's poetry. Boscán made the division in this way because he envisioned his poetic development in three stages: a medieval period of *cancionero* poetry, which is Book One; an early Renaissance period of Petrarchan sonnets and *canciones,* which constitutes Book Two; and a later Renaissance period of Humanistic poetry, found in Book Three, which contains a short epic, a Horatian epistle, and an Italian "Capitolo," "Epistola," and "Ottava rima." These three books are therefore studied here in the same order and comprise the material in Chapters Two, Three, and Four. Chapter Five summarizes the principal contributions of Boscán to the rise of Spanish Renaissance poetry and demonstrates his importance in the shift from a medieval world view to a Renaissance one. Following the usual notes and selected bibliography are three appendixes that will aid the non-Hispanic reader to appreciate more fully the milieu in which Boscán worked. The first one is my translation of the poet's important manifesto on the adoption of the new Italian meters. The second appendix is my translation of a poem written by Crostóbal de Castillejo against the new meters; it shows clearly just how strong the opposition was to what Boscán and Garcilaso had set out to do. The third document is the text and my translation of Boscán's most important early poem, "Boscán's Conversion." It was too long to include within the body of Chapter Two, but it was likewise too important to be omitted.

A number of other things have been omitted, however. Over the centuries, some minor pieces by the poet not included in the first editions of his *Works* have been discovered and edited. The most important poems are eighteen *coplas,* an Italianate *canción,* and a piece entitled "Capítulo II." Some of this poetry is of doubtful authenticity; and since Boscán did not include any of them in his original anthology, he must have considered them either unworthy or inappropriate. None, to be truthful, is of outstanding artistic merit. Another item omitted from this Twayne book is Boscán's translation of Baldassare Castiglione's *Il cortegiano,* although that work is referred to often because of its value in enunciating the new Platonic philosophy that Boscán embraces after the early 1530s. To undertake a thorough examination of *The Courtier* here would have meant a separate chapter and would actually have been more a study of Castiglione's thought and style than of Boscán's. The final item omitted is a curious rewriting of Boscán's lyrics by Sebastián de Córdoba entitled *Las obras de Boscán y Garcilaso trasladadas en materias christianas y religiosas* (Granada: René Rabut, 1575; republished Zaragoza: Juan Soler, 1577). Córdoba takes the Catalan's poems and rewords them to impart a religious sense. The volume is assuredly an important contribution to Counter-Reformation "a lo divino" (religious) poetry, but it has little value for interpreting Boscán's original intentions. It can be consulted in

Preface

a modern edition by Glen R. Gale (Ann Arbor: University of Michigan, 1971).

The edition used throughout this study is *Las obras de Juan Boscán, repartidas en tres libros,* ed. William I. Knapp (Madrid: Librería de M. Murillo, 1875). Although a number of equally good renditions have appeared since 1875, Knapp's remains the standard one cited by critics in the field and it is the edition that preceding scholars have consistently employed. The only drawback to Knapp's version is that Spanish accentuation and punctuation have changed somewhat in the past hundred years. In this Twayne monograph the punctuation remains the same, but the accentuation has been modernized. No other alterations, orthographic or otherwise, were thought to be necessary. Finally, all translations are the author's. They strive to be as literal as possible, even to the point, regretfully, of sometimes being vague and twisted in syntax in English; but it was felt that the non-Hispanic reader would prefer a faithful word by word, line by line rendition to a freer, more poetically sensitive one.

DAVID H. DARST

Tallahassee, Florida

Chronology

CHAPTER 1

The Life and Times of Juan Boscán

I Childhood and Education

J UAN Boscán Almugáver was the son of Juan Valentín Boschá,
a public official for the city of Barcelona, and of Violante
Almugáver.[1] Boscán's precise date of birth is not known, but there
is a document from 1493 that refers to him as an infant. Another
document dated 1506 declares Boscán to be less than twenty years
old, and a 1512 manifest presents his age as between twenty and
twenty-five. Juan Boscán thus had to be born to Juan Valentín and
Violante sometime between 1487 and 1492, probably closer to the
latter.

Juan Valentín Boschá, the poet's father, was the son of Juan
Francisco Boschá (d. 1480), a historian and author of the *Annales
Urbis Barcinonensis*. Violante Almugáver was the daughter of Juan
Almugáver. The Boschá and Almugáver families were close even
before the marriage of Juan Valentín and Violante, because in 1473
Violante's father took as his second wife Juan Valentín's sister,
Marquesa Boschá. Both families were long-time citizens of Bar-
celona and had many patronymic relatives in the government and
political circles. Boscán's parents were married in 1480 and, besides
Juan, had two daughters. Violante, the eldest child, married Felipe
de Ferrera; and Leonor married Bernardo de So.

Juan Valentín died in 1492, the terminus ad quem for the poet's
birth. The child thus grew up under the protection of his mother,
his paternal uncle Beltrán Boschá, and Guillermo Ramón de Vall.
The family lived from a number of annuities granted the widow by
the city of Barcelona and the Crown of Aragon.

Perhaps as early as 1507,[2] Juan Boscán left Barcelona to take up
permanent residence at the court of Ferdinand and Isabel. If he did

not go in 1507, he probably went in 1510, when a relative of his, Francisco Boscá, was knighted by King Ferdinand. Positive proof of residence there does not come until 1514, when Boscán is mentioned as an *alumno* of Ferdinand V. That same year Lucio Marineo Sículo published an *Epistolarum familiarum* that included an exchange of formal letters with his student Juan Boscán. For some reason this is the only reference to Boscán's relationship to the man who must have introduced him to the Italian, Roman, and Greek classics and who must have been the major intellectual guide to the young poet.

Lucas di Marinis[3] was born in 1444 in Vizzini, Sicily; and, incredible as it may seem, he did not learn to read or write until he was twenty-five years old. He studied in Palermo and later became tutor to the children of Lucas Pullastra. He then traveled to Rome, where he latinized his name to Lucius Marineus. In 1479 he returned to Palermo, where in 1481 he happened to meet Fadrique Enríquez (d. 1538), son of the Spanish admiral Alfonso Enríquez. This Fadrique will become admiral in 1485 at his father's death and will later participate in a poetic debate on fidelity with Juan Boscán.

In 1484 don Fadrique returned to Spain, taking Marineo with him; and in October of the same year the Sicilian was offered the chair of poetry and oratory at Salamanca. He remained there for twelve years and became a close friend of two other great Spanish humanists, Peter Martyr (Pietro Martire d'Anghiera) and Antonio de Nebrija. In 1496 Marineo went to the Spanish court to aid Peter Martyr with the education of the nobility's children. He remained there until his death around 1533. Among his writings are *De Hispaniae Laudibus* (1495), *De Primis Aragoniae Regibus* (1509), and *De Rebus Hispaniae Memorabilibus* (1533).

From Marineo the young Juan Boscán would receive the knowledge necessary to translate the Italian love poetry, as well as Latin and Greek lyrics, into Spanish. But of course Marineo was not the only link between Spain and the Italo-Greco-Roman culture. Strong cultural relations between Spain and Italy had existed throughout the Middle Ages,[4] and they crystalized in 1443 when Alfonso of Aragón (reigned 1416–1458) captured and retained the kingdom of Naples from the house of Anjou. Alfonso willed the kingdom of Naples to his bastard son, Ferrante I, and left Aragón to his brother, Juan II. The familial ties were further bound by

Ferrante's marriage in 1477 to Juana, his uncle Juan's daughter and cousin Ferdinand the Catholic's sister. Meanwhile, the Spaniard Alfonso Borgia had ascended to the Papal See as Calixto III (reigned 1455–1458). He put his family into power throughout Italy, and was followed at the end of the century by his nephew Rodrigo Borgia, who took the name Alexander VI (reigned 1495–1503). This latter pope had the dubious honor of fathering the notorious Cesare and Lucrezia Borgia. Two other sons, Pedro Luis and Juan, were dukes of Gandía and powerful figures in Valencian politics. A clear example of the Hispano-Italian interchange is that nineteen of the forty-three cardinals named by Alexander VI were Spanish.

In 1503 Spanish hegemony was again felt in Neopolitan governmental circles. The French king Charles VIII had tried to wrest the throne from the young Ferrante II, and Gonzalo de Córdoba entered the kingdom to protect the Crown. King Ferdinand then decided to retain Naples for himself and brought Ferrante to Spain to keep him out of the way. In 1506 the Catholic King married Germaine de Foix—Isabel had died in 1504—and went to Naples to solidify his authority there. Lucio Marineo accompanied him; and we can suppose that Juan Boscán, if by then he was at court, also made the journey.

Better documented is Boscán's participation, along with that of Garcilaso de la Vega, in the abortive attempt by the Spanish navy to relieve the Isle of Rhodes from Turkish invasion in 1522. Boscán was by this time in the service of Fernando Alvarez de Toledo, Duke of Alba (1508–1582), as tutor and companion. This same duke later became regent in the Netherlands under Philip II, where he set up the infamous "Court of Blood." He is likewise accredited with permitting the wholesale slaughter of the citizens of Lisbon when the city was seized by Spain in 1580. Also fully documented is Boscán's journey to Germany in 1532 with the Duke of Alba and Charles I to help Vienna repulse the Turks; but by this time Boscán had been writing verses in the Italian manner for six years.

II *Introduction of the Italianate Style*

As a preface to his Italianate verses in Book Two of his *Works,* Boscán inserted a letter to the Duchess of Somma (see Appendix A for a translation). He explained therein how he was first persuaded to write in the new meters by one Andrea Navaggiero, the Venetian ambassador to Spain. The momentous conversation took place in Granada some time between June and December, 1526. Boscán and Navaggiero were by then good friends, because the ambassador had been at the Spanish court since June of 1525, and the two were of about the same age. Navaggiero was born in Venice in 1483,[4] so he was only four to eight years the senior to Boscán, who would be around thirty-five. Navaggiero also had undertaken an excellent preparation in the classics. He studied in Venice with Sabellicus, in Padua with Marcus Mosurus, and in Pardenone at the home of Bartholomeo of Alviano. In 1506 he succeeded Sabellicus as librarian of Saint Mark's and remained in that position until he was named ambassador to Spain. Navaggiero was a gifted editor of Greek texts, publishing at the Aldine Press the works of Cicero and Ovid (both with long prefaces), Terence, Lucretius, Virgil, Horace, Tibullus, and Quintilian. It could have occurred to no better-prepared humanist, then, to persuade the likewise humanistically oriented Juan Boscán to write in the Italian meters.

Navaggiero's life after his momentous conversation with Boscán was not so fortuitous. In 1526 Pope Clement VII (Giulio de Medici) formed the League of Cognac — sometimes called the Clementine League — with Venice, Milan, and France against Spain. The following year Spanish and German troops sacked Rome and took the pope prisoner. The fall of Rome caused Venice, France, and England to declare war on Spain; and Navaggiero was ordered to return to his homeland. Charles retained the ambassador in the village of Poza de la Sal until his own ministries should be restored safely to Spain, so Navaggiero did not leave the country until May of 1528. He was immediately sent to France by his government to aid in the war against Spain, but he died unexpectedly the next year on May 8 in Blois.

What Navaggiero wanted Boscán to do was a very simple thing: to write verses with eleven syllables rather than with eight, this latter number being the usual Spanish line. All the poetry in Book One, for example, is in eight-syllable verses, while all of the poetry in Books Two and Three is in eleven-syllable verses (the Italianate *canciones,* naturally, have lines with seven and eleven syllables). These new forms include the sonnet, *canción, terza rima, ottava rima,* and blank verse; and Boscán — or his friend Garcilaso de la Vega — was the first Spaniard to attempt successfully the application of these modes to Spanish poetry. It is certain that many writers before Boscán had attempted to compose verses in some of these forms, but the only one who merits homage is Iñigo López de Mendoza, Marqués de Santillana, who had written forty-two "Sonetos fechos al itálico modo."

In order to perceive clearly the momentous task Juan Boscán undertook when he decided to write with Italian meters, it is necessary to understand the nature of the various poetic modes prevalent in Spain at the beginning of the sixteenth century. The first and most important strain was the *cancionero* tradition, so-called because of the title given to the poetic anthologies in the fifteenth century. The most famous is the *Cancionero de Baena,* compiled by Juan de Baena in 1445 for King John II of Castile. Its most notable contributors were Alfonso Alvarez de Villasandino, the Galician troubadour Macías, Juan Rodríguez del Padrón, Francisco Imperial, and Juan Alvarez Gato. The poetry is in general courtly and aristocratic, continuing thereby in Spanish the amorous lyrics of the Provençal-Galician school. Another influential songbook was the Aragonese *Cancionero de Stúñiga,* containing poems written during the reign of Alfonso V (1396–1458). It shows a stronger Italian influence, and its most accomplished authors are Pedro Torrellas and Juan de Dueñas. The culmination of this tradition is the enormous *Cancionero general,* anthologized in 1511 by Hernando de Castillo and republished several times in the sixteenth century.

In all of these songbooks the short-lined poems — *arte menor* — predominate over the twelve syllable line — *arte mayor* — and in all of them the attitude toward love is decidedly medieval. Given that by the beginning of the sixteenth century outside influences from Petrarch and the *dolce stil nuovo,* from the dying Provençal tradition, and from the Catalan poets Ausias March and Jordi de Sant Jordi begin to seep into the Castilian foundation, the medieval love tradition remains firm. The courtly ambience of this Castilian poetry has been precisely described by Rafael Lapesa: "Love is conceived as a cult and a service; this spiritual vassalage dignifies the lover, separating him from vile thoughts and infusing in him desire for excellence. The poetry explores, more or less scholastically, the galleries of the soul, underlining the contrasts between reason and desire, between objective vision of the world and the personal focus of the individual. Sadness and spiritual instability are the daughters of the interior struggle and the shy comportment of the beloved. The lovers give in to their pain, take pleasure relishing the suffering, and savor with gratification the tears they shed. Nevertheless, this pleasure of the *martire* does not impede their relating endlessly the years of servitude."[6]

Concurrent with this same tradition is the poetry of Ausias March, who influenced Boscán's poetry more than anyone other than Petrarch. A Catalan born in 1397 near Valencia, March wrote Provençal unrhymed verses called *estramps,* filled with the intense expression of his search for a pure and spiritual love.[7] His *Cants de Amor* are almost all directed to a married woman named Teresa, to whom he pours out his pain and suffering. There is a metaphysical side to the torment, however; for March believes, as do all true courtly lovers, that the anguish is a cathartic agent that cleanses the body, allowing thereby the soul freer range of sublime experience.

The second current that most influences Boscán is the Petrarchan tradition, for it is from Francesco Petrarca that the Spaniard received all the formal elements of his new poetry: the sonnet, *terza rima, canción,* as well as the new tone that came with the hendecasyllabic verse. Both of these formal aspects will be discussed in Chapter Three; but it is necessary to emphasize here the special attitude toward love as a development of spiritual maturity that Boscán inherited from Petrarch. Rafael Lapesa describes it succinctly: "The slow discourse of hendecasyllables and heptasyllables repudiated the direct expression and the picturesque realism frequent in the *cancioneros;* on the other hand, it was the suitable rhythm for the exploration of one's ego in detailed analysis, and for expressing the contemplative rapture before nature. These were the two great themes of the new school. Petrarch had given the model for the scrutiny of states of the soul. The poets, upon exploring their own spirit, became conscious of themselves and contributed thus to the discovery of the individual, the principal feat of the Renaissance."[8]

Other poetic traditions that existed in Spain contemporary with Boscán had little direct influence. The only literary current disputed among scholars, in fact, is the use of the hendecasyllable. The eleven-syllable rhyme had of course existed throughout the Middle Ages in Spain, and no one ever considered Boscán to be the very first to write a line with that number of syllables in it. Cristóbal de Castillejo pointed out that Juan de Mena used the hendecasyllable, and Argote de Molina claimed Don Juan Manuel to be the first Spaniard to use it.[9] The most primitive form is a French decasyllable with the accent on the fourth syllable and sometimes a second beat at the seventh syllable. It is used in the *Chanson de Roland,* in early Provençal verse, and in Catalan poetry all the way up to the fifteenth century. The Spanish equivalent of this form with the accent on the fourth syllable is found in the *Poema de mío Cid,* in Don Juan Manuel's *El Conde Lucanor,* in the archpriest of Hita's *Libro de buen amor,* and in Enrique de Villena's *Arte de trovar.* A Galician form appeared early in the thirteenth century and was used by Alfonso the Wise in his *Cantigas de Santa María* and by the troubadour writers whose works appear in the songbooks referred to as *Vaticano, Colocci Brancuti,* and *Ajuda.* This Galician verse is similar to the Provençal one, but has a hard caesura after the fourth or fifth syllable.

The most popular form of the hendecasyllable in Spain, however, is the one where the accent falls on the sixth syllable. The accent is found there in Juan de Mena, Francisco Imperial, and the Marqués de Santillana; yet all these writers before Boscán have a tendency to regress to the "medieval" pattern of placing the stress on the fourth or fifth syllable. Boscán intentionally avoids these early forms of the hendecasyllable and practices the Petrarchan style of placing accents on the sixth syllable or on the fourth and eighth syllables.

Despite these precedents to Boscán's verse forms, the poet had a legitimate right to consider himself the first Spaniard to use Italian meters. In the dedicatory letter to the Duchess of Somma (see Appendix A for the translation; the Spanish text is pp. 165–73 in the Knapp edition) that Boscán published as an introduction to Book Two, which contains the Italianate sonnets and *canciones,* Boscán justifies his role as the inventor of the new verses ("inventor destas trovas") in Spain. He explains that he indeed is the first Spaniard to use Italianate meters ("He querido ser el primero que ha juntado la lengua castellana con el modo de escribir italiano"). He did not invent them just to be known as their inventor, however, but only as a way to spend idle time. In fact, the idea was not his at all, but Andrea Navaggiero's. When the two were in Granada in the summer of 1526, Navaggiero not only directly asked, relates Boscán, but even begged the poet to try composing Spanish verses with Italian meters. Boscán says he tried out the new rhymes, but would have dropped the project if Garcilaso de la Vega had not urged him to continue by praising his work and offering his own examples.

At this point in the new enterprise, Boscán continues, he also began to doubt whether the Castilian meters he had been using for so long were as good as the new Italian ones with which he was experimenting. For one thing, the eight-syllable line characteristic of Spanish verse had no origin except in the popular poetry of the masses, which certainly gave it little authority to be honored. The Italian eleven-syllable verse, on the other hand, had well-founded origins which showed its flexibility and authority ("Porque en él vemos, donde quiera que se nos muestra, una disposición muy capaz para recibir qualquier materia, o grave, o sotil, o dificultosa, o fácil, y así mismo para ayuntarse con qualquier estilo de los que hallamos entre los autores antiguos aprobados").

Petrarch, Boscán relates, was the first in Italy to perfect the hendecasyllable; and all later authors, including Boscán, follow his lead. Dante also used it very well; and, at the same time or a little earlier, the Provençal poets were employing it. Among these Provençal writers were many Catalans, and Boscán singles out for special consideration Ausias March.[10] Before the Provençal poets the same form, keeping in mind the difference in languages, was popular among the Latins, who got it from the Greeks. With such an authoritative tradition, concludes the poet, this new verse form is worthy not only of being received by a language so good as Castilian, but even of being preferred in that language over all the popular verses ("De manera que este género de trovas, y con la autoridad de su valor propio, y con la reputación de los antiguos y modernos que le han usado, es dino, no solamente de ser recibido de una lengua tan buena como es la castellana, mas aún de ser en ella preferido a todos los versos vulgares"). Boscán therefore recommends the meters to all Spanish poets, and hopes they and the duchess will remember that while his own verses are not the best, they at least have served their purpose by being the first.

Thus runs the argument of the major portion of Boscán's letter. Throughout, the poet valiantly admits the newness of what he has done, and he brazenly declares that it is better than anything ever written in the native meters. But Boscán is also very defensive about his invention. At the beginning of his letter to the duchess, he asserts the superiority of the Italian style over his native Castilian verses ("La manera destas es más grave y de más artificio, y, si yo no me engaño, mucho mejor que la de las otras"); but in the next sentence he admits that he knew he would have many detractors. What he did not expect was that the opponents would be so vociferous in their complaints. He explains how they attacked him with arguments that the consonantal rhyme was not as good as with Castilian verses ("que en las trovas desta arte los consonantes no andaban tan descubiertas, ni sonaban tanto como en las castellanas"), that the verse form was too prosaic ("que este verso no sabían si era verso, o si era prosa"), and that the poetry was only fit for women because it was so sweet and feminine ("que esto principalmente había de ser para mugeres, y que ellas no curaban de cosas de sustancia, sino del son de las palabras, y de la dulzura del consonante"). Boscán therewith refutes each of these arguments by denouncing as unsophisticated the obvious rhyme schemes of Castilian poetry, by defending the intellectual capacity of women, and by condemning the prosaic, hard-sounding poetry of the *Cancionero general*. It is only after this strong defense of his poetry and the condemnation of his critics that Boscán finds the nerve to describe in detail how he came upon the verses.

Boscán's defensive nature was certainly justified. The detractors of the new style must have begun their attack as soon as manuscript copies of the Catalan's poetry began to be circulated. The most famous assault on the new meters came shortly after Boscán's death, but it could have been written much earlier. I refer of course to the "Censure of Spanish Poets Who Write with Italian Meters" (see Appendix B for a full translation) by Cristóbal de Castillejo (1492?-1550). It was published by Alonso de Ulloa in the Venice, 1553, edition of Boscán's works, and it immediately became an anthology piece. Castillejo ingeniously sees the new group of poets as a protestant sect of heretics against which the Inquisition should be implemented.[11] He calls up the remarks of the ghosts of Juan de Mena, Jorge Manrique, Garci Sánchez de Badajoz, Pedro de Cartagena, and Bartolomé de Torres Naharro when they learn that a new verse has been introduced into Spain. Castillejo then inserts a delightful sonnet about how Garcilaso and Boscán arrive at the isle of departed spirits and surprise all the troubadours there because the two are dressed as Spaniards but speak Italian. He then strikes out harshly against the new "foreign" form, especially Boscán's own statement that the Italian verses are more elegant and have greater authority than the native variety.

At the midpoint of the poem (which has two hundred and thirty lines in the traditional verse known as *décimas*), Castillejo returns to the reactions of the troubadours, who desire to hear examples of the new verses. Castillejo inserts a sonnet by Boscán and an *ottava rima* by Garcilaso de la Vega into his poem, to present subsequently the reactions of Mena, Manrique, Garci Sánchez, Cartagena, and Torres Naharro to the new poetry. Characteristically, they are no longer surprised by the verses because, according to Castillejo and his cohorts, they had used the same hendecasyllabic forms in their own poetry. The poem ends with the departed spirits assigning one of their number to write a sonnet lauding the new forms, since they are worthy of praise if only out of courtesy and for the sake of recognizing their true Hispanic origins:

> Al cabo la conclusión
> fué que por buena crîança
> y por honrar la invención
> de parte de la nación
> Sean dignas de alabança.

Despite the vehement attacks against the Italian meters, the new forms immediately became the predominant style for elegant and erudite poetry. In 1546, only two years after the publication of Boscán's and Garcilaso's poetry, Ambrosio de Morales wrote of Boscán: "He made our poetry not owe anything in diversity and majesty to the Italian compositions, being in the refinement of the ideas equal to them, and not inferior in expressing the ideas and having them understood, as some of the Italians themselves confess."[12] A short three years later, Bernardino Daza Pinciano began translating Andrea Alciati's *Emblemata* from Latin and decided to use Italian meters (tercets and sonnets) for the translations into Spanish. In the preface he explains why he chose the new meters: "But whatever the case, all the verses printed in that final edition I translated in the Italian manner, and that is what I meant to signify when I called them *rhimas,* for that is what the Italians call their *coplas.* I did this because I saw that you gave more attention to that manner of verse because it was more artistic, and likewise more appropriate, because in very few verses I said more than with the other Castilian verse forms, which you all now call *redondillas.*"[13]

A final aspect of Boscán's new style is the question of artistry. The poet hints throughout his letter to the Duchess of Somma that the Italian verses have a greater fluidity, a greater softness, a greater ease of expression than do the harsh Castilian meters. He is writing the letter in 1542, long after he has dominated all the new meters, and he thus has years of experience to prove his thesis. He has also become imbued with the current Neoplatonic spirit, gained principally from his translating Baldassare Castiglione's *Il cortegiano.* In the first book of that work, the author presents a complete discourse on the purpose of art, and what he says jibes perfectly with Boscán's feelings on the subject. Count Ludovico de Canossa, who is the speaker in this part of the dialogued novel, begins to describe the grace needed by a courtier to be perfect, and explains: "But, having thought many times already about how this grace is acquired (leaving aside those who have it from the stars), I have found quite a universal rule which in this matter seems to me valid above all others, and in all human affairs whether in word or deed: and that is to avoid affectation in every way possible as though it were some very rough and dangerous reef; and (to pronounce a new word perhaps) to practice in all things a certain *sprezzatura* [nonchalance], so as to conceal all art and make whatever is done or said appear to be without effort and almost without any thought about it."[14]

This passage describes magnificently the type of elegance that is exhibited in Boscán's later lyrics. One gets the impression — which is patently false — that the poet simply scribbled off hurriedly the long poem "Leandro y Hero" and the festival piece "Octava rima." Such is of course not the case, and the fact that they appear to have been so effortlessly written is proof by Renaissance standards of their consummate artistry. The inspiration for this attempt at *disinvoltura,* or ease, is classical literature, as Count Ludovico notes: "I remember having read of certain most excellent orators in ancient times who, among the other things they did, tried to make everyone believe that they had no knowledge whatever of letters; and, dissembling their knowledge, they made their orations appear to be composed in the simplest manner and according to the dictates of nature and truth rather than of effort and art" (pp. 43–44).

Boscán's success in writing "effortless" verse in the Italian manner marks him undisputedly as a Renaissance man.

III   *The Later Years*

By pure happenstance, this other Italian who influenced so profoundly Juan Boscán's literary thought was also an ambassador to Spain. Count Baldassare Castiglione (1478–1529)[15] came to Spain in March of 1525 as the papal nuncio of Clement VII, the Medici pope so detested by King Charles. To make matters more unpleasant for Castiglione, he arrived on the very day that the Spanish populace learned of the overwhelming victory of Pavia and the capture of the French monarch. When Navaggiero, one of Castiglione's oldest friends, arrived in June, the count must have greeted him with open arms. From that moment until Navaggiero's departure, the two Italians were constantly together.

In 1526 Castiglione learned that his patroness Elisabetta of Urbino had died, and he decided to publish in her memory *Il cortegiano*. He had written it between 1523–24, but the conversations that make up the book had taken place in Urbino years earlier. He asked Navaggiero to help him with the final draft, and sent the manuscript to the Venetian's son-in-law, Giovanni Ramusio, to be published at the Aldine Press. The volume was printed in 1528 under the supervision of Ramusio and Cardinal Bembo. At this time the count's fortunes in the Spanish court improved. Late in 1528 Clement changed sides from the French to the Spanish, and offered to crown Charles as emperor of the Holy Roman Empire. Castiglione was instrumental in arranging Charles's visit to Italy, and the Spanish monarch gave the bishopric of Avila to him in February, 1529, as recompense. Two days later, however, on February 7, Castiglione suddenly died. His body was taken to Italy and interred at a monastery near Padua.

Juan Boscán must have known Castiglione well, and he must have talked to the count numerous times about poetry and other matters, especially since Castiglione was in Granada in 1526 with Navaggiero. It was not until April 2, 1534, however, that Boscán's translation of *Il cortegiano* appeared. Entitled *Los cuatro libros del cortesano, compuestos en italiano por el conde Baltasar Castellón, y agora nuevamente traducidos en lengua castellana por Boscán* (Barcelona: Pedro Monpezat, 1534), the work was a resounding success and found its way into the library of every educated Spaniard. Other editions appeared in 1539 (Toledo), 1540 (Salamanca: Pedro Tovans), 1544 (Antwerp: Martín Nucio, who also published numerous editions of Boscán's poetry), 1553 (Zaragoza: Miguel de Zapila), 1561 (Antwerp: Martín Nucio), 1569 (Valladolid: Francisco Fernández de Córdoba), and 1573 (Antwerp: Philip Nucio).[16] Remarkably, there are no more printings of the book until the scholarly edition of Antonio María Fabié (Madrid: Librería de los Bibliófilos, 1873). *El cortesano* was a typical Renaissance work expressing typical Renaissance values, and the absence of printings after 1573 indicates conclusively the change in intellectual climate that came with the Counter-Reformation and the baroque style.

El cortesano is prefaced by two letters (pp. 5–15 in the Fabié edition) to Doña Gerónima Palova de Almogáver, the wife of Boscán's first cousin Juan Almugáver. The first letter is from Boscán and explains how he decided to translate *El cortesano*. The second one is by none other than Garcilaso de la Vega.

Boscán explains in his introductory epistle that a short time earlier Garcilaso de la Vega had sent him a copy of *Il cortegiano*. The Catalan immediately sat down to read it, and he was so impressed by its contents and style that he decided therewith to translate it into Spanish. He then explains precisely how he went about translating the piece, stressing that he is not simply putting the book into Spanish, a task that would require no skill. Rather he is going to give a free oratorical translation of the work ("Traducir este libro no es propiamente *romanzarle,* sino *mudarle* de una lengua vulgar en otra quizá tan buena").[17] Boscán follows this statement with a paean to Doña Gerónima, but he returns to the subject again, as if he could not get the matter of "translating" versus "switching languages" off his mind. He admits that he has not tried to translate it word for word ("sacarle palabra por palabra"), but instead has taken the liberty to change and even to suppress parts ("de mudarla o de callarla"). Nevertheless, he fears that much of it may not sound well in Spanish.

Garcilaso's letter expresses the same attitude towards translations and translating as Boscán's does. He remarks to Doña Gerónima that he did not think he could convince his friend to do a translation because Boscán despised translators ("le vía siempre aborrecerse con los que romanzan libros"). Boscán did such a good job, Garcilaso later adds, that the book reads as if it were originally written in Spanish, because the poet avoided affectation, dryness, archaic words, and neologisms; of more importance, he did not let himself be bound by the strict meaning of the Italian version, but translated instead the general sense of the work ("fue, demás desto, muy fiel traductor, porque no se ató al rigor de la letra, como hacen algunos, sino a la verdad de las sentencias"). And finally, Boscán voiced magnificently the different manners of speech of the various speakers in the book, which was the most difficult part of the translation.

The strangest remarks in these letters, however, have nothing to do with translations. Boscán avers that he did not know of the existence of *Il cortegiano* until he received a copy from Garcilaso in 1533, and Garcilaso substantiates Boscán's explanation in his own letter. Yet it is difficult to believe that a man who saw both Navaggiero and Castiglione almost daily during their writing of the final draft in 1526–28 would not have known of the existence of *Il cortegiano* until five years later. Moreover, Boscán was in Italy and Germany in 1532; and he might have also accompanied Charles, along with Garcilaso de la Vega, to the Congress of Bologna in 1529 and to the siege of Florence in 1530. One can only suppose that Boscán knew and had even read *Il cortegiano* long before he received a copy from Garcilaso in 1533. He evidently chose to remain silent about any earlier acquaintance with the work either because he did not want to hurt Garcilaso's feelings — who, as can be seen from the tone of his letter, was quite excited about his role in the translation and publication of the volume — or because it was only in 1533 at Garcilaso's urging that it occurred to him to translate the work into Spanish.

In the same year of 1533, according to a letter written by the Duke of Alba, Boscán was preparing to marry Ana Girón de Rebolledo of Valencia. The actual marriage document is not signed until 1539, when Boscán would have been between forty-seven and fifty-two years old and his wife, who was born between 1514 and 1519, would have been from twenty to twenty-five years of age. Now Boscán fathered three daughters by Ana Girón: Mariana, Beatriz, and Violante. Boscán passed away September 21, 1542, after taking ill at Perpiñan, where he had gone with the Duke of Alba. This means that Ana Girón had to bear three live children in less than four years, which is quite a difficult thing to do. It may be, but there is no proof, that in 1533 Juan Boscán and Ana Girón de Rebolledo indeed married and began living together; but that they did not sign the official matrimonial papers until August 7, 1539. This hypothesis puts Boscán's age between forty-one and forty-six, when he would be more sexually active, and Ana Girón's age between fourteen and nineteen, which is closer to the age when girls actually got married in the Renaissance.

Boscán was preparing his poetry for publication when he died. In the Preface to the Reader ("A los lectores," pp. 3–5 in the Knapp edition), Ana Girón explains that shortly before his death Boscán's friends finally persuaded him to publish some of his poems ("Este libro consintió Boscán que se imprimiese, forzado de los ruegos de muchos"). He undertook the publication for two reasons. For one, he began to worry that an unauthorized version of his verses might appear ("que, sin su voluntad, no se adelantase otro a imprimirlo"). The other reason was more scholarly. Boscán's works had evidently become so popular that there were scores of manuscripts of his verses being copied and passed around throughout Europe.[18] The large number of variants and errors bothered his poetic sensibility, so he decided to publish the definitive edition ("y también porque se acabasen los yerros que en los traslados que le hurtaban había, que eran infinitos"). Before his death, continues his wife, Boscán had already divided the volume into four books and had written the dedicatory letter to the Duchess of Somma. Ana Girón further states that although she knows that her husband would have made numerous changes in the manuscript, she has decided to publish the works exactly as he left them, since even that form will be better than the chaotic state of his poems in the various manuscripts ("y así se ha tenido por menor inconveniente que se imprimiesen como estaban, y que gozásedes todos dellas, aunque no estén en la perfición en que estuvieran como Boscán las pusiera, que no por haber quedado acabadas de su mano, tenerlas guardadas y escondidas donde nunca pareciesen, sino tan mal concertadas y escritas, como suelen andar por ahí de mano").

The volume appeared March 20, 1543, printed by Garles Amorós in Barcelona with the title *Las obras de Boscán y algunas de Garcilaso de la Vega repartidas en quatro libros*.[19] This *editio princeps* was quickly followed in November by a pirated Lisbon printing with the same title by Luis Rodríguez, and by a reprinting of the *princeps* in August of the following year by Pedro de Castro in Medina del Campo. Also in 1544 an edition appeared in Antwerp,

Belgium, by Martín Nucio, which included a number of new poems (the "Conversión de Boscán," "Mar de amor," and twelve *coplas*) and which was reprinted by the Nucio press at least four times. These early editions were followed by others in 1547 (Lyons: Juan Frellon, and Rome: Antonio de Salamanca), 1548 (Paris: Lazaro de Ocaña), 1549 (Lyons: Juan Frellon), 1553 (Valladolid: Juan María de Terranova y Jacome de Liarcay, and Venice: Gabriel Giolito de Ferrar y sus hermanos), 1554 (Barcelona: Garles Amorós, and Antwerp: Juan Steelsio), 1555 (Estella: Andrian de Anverez), 1558? (Toledo: Juan Ferrer), 1575 (Alcalá de Henares: Sebastián Martínez), 1576 (Antwerp: Pedro Bellero, reprinted in 1597), and 1658 (Lyons: Juan Antonio Hugetan y Marco Antonio Revaud, a reprinting of the Frellon 1549 edition). The next edition does not appear for over two hundred years, when William I. Knapp published *Las obras de Juan Boscán repartidas en tres libros* (Madrid: M. Murillo, 1875), which is, by the way, the first edition ever published solely of Boscán's opera. The other recent publications of Boscán's works are a reprinting of the complete 1543 edition by F.S.R. (Madrid: Aguilar, 1944) and *Obras poéticas,* ed. Martín de Riquer, Antonio Coma, and Joaquín Molas (Barcelona: Facultad de Filosofía y Letras, 1957).

In sum, Boscán's and Garcilaso's poetry saw over twenty printings in twenty-five short years; but after 1569, quite oddly, only four more printings appeared. The reason that the reading public lost interest so quickly in Boscán's poetry is all too apparent. It was actually Garcilaso de la Vega's verses that were in demand; and so when in 1569 the Salamancan bookseller Simón Borgoñón initiated the printing of Garcilaso's poetry apart from Boscán's, he immediately and permanently cut off demand for the Catalan's writings.[20] The volume that precipitated the divorce of Garcilaso from Boscán was *Las obras del excelente poeta Garcilaso de la Vega, agora nuevamente corregidas de muchos errores que en todas las impressiones passadas avía* (Salamanca: Mathías Gast, 1569). This work, in effect, became the new *editio princeps* for Garcilaso's poetry, for it was the edition consulted by the later commentators and publishers rather than Book Four of *Las obras de Boscán y algunas de Garcilasso de la Vega.*

CHAPTER 2

The First Book: Castilian Poetry

BOOK One of Juan Boscán's poetry in the 1543 princeps edition comprises two *villancicos,* nineteen *coplas,* and six Castilian *canciones,* although not in that order. It also has an introductory poem in hendecasyllabic blank verse directed to the Duchess of Somma that is a direct imitation of a Catullus lyric that begins "Quio dono lepidum novum libellum." Since Boscán assuredly wrote his dedicatory piece specifically as the proem to his works, "A la Duquesa de Somma" is probably the last poem he wrote for the volume. In the Antwerp, 1544, edition of Boscán's works, the contents of Book One are expanded by the addition of twelve more *coplas* and two long poems entitled "Conversión de Boscán" and "Mar de amor."

I *Villancicos*

The first *villancico* is perhaps one of the most beautiful and best organized poems in Boscán's corpus, and it will serve as a good example of the courtly love theme that permeates the lyrics in Book One. Moreover, the *villancico* is the first piece in the body of Book One, coming immediately after the dedicatory verses to Somma. It is a short ten-line poem rhyming abbcdcddbb, with its lines in eight syllables. Two of the lines, however, have only four syllables each; that is, they are in *pie quebrado.* The poem thus fulfills the normal format of a *villancico,* which calls for a three-line *cabeza,* a *pie* of four lines, a two-line *mudanza,* and a final *retornelo* that repeats the first line.[1] It was meant to be sung to the accompaniment of a harp or guitar, for there exists a sixteenth-century songbook in which this lyric has been set to music.[2]

The literary merit of the poem is exemplary for its adherence to

31

the "negative paradox" in courtly poetry, where all the statements about the poet's love are expressed in the conditional tense and negatively: if A had not occurred, B would not have occurred either.

Villancico I

Si no os hubiera mirado,
no penara;
pero tampoco os mirara.
Veros harto mal ha sido,
mas no veros peor fuera;
no quedara tan perdido,
pero mucho más perdiera.
¿Qué viera aquél que no os viera?
¿Quál quedara,
Señora, si no os mirara?   (p. 123)

(If I had not seen you,
I would not suffer;
but I would not see you either.
To see you has been enough anguish,
but not to see you would have been worse;
I would not be so lost
but I would have lost much more.
What would one see who could not see you?
What would remain,
Lady, if one could not see you?)

(As stated in the Preface, page numbers are those of the Knapp edition of Boscán's *Obras*.)

The whole poem is thus structured around "no," which occurs in six of the ten lines, and the verbs "mirar" and "ver," which together appear seven times (two infinitives and five conditionals). The emphasis on sight as the medium of love is of course characteristic of courtly ardor, for beauty enters through the eyes and makes its way into the heart.[3] The poet brilliantly utilizes this idea by placing his whole raison d'être on sight and on the contemplation of his lady; for, if he could not see her, absolutely nothing would remain. The singer thus finds himself caught in the courtly paradox of suffering incredible pain because he saw her, but being now aware as well that seeing her has given purpose to his existence.

Technically, the *villancico* is exquisitely organized. The "si" which begins it affects the entire composition, because it forces the conditional tense to be used throughout. The poet expresses the paradox of "if not A, then not B" in the first three verses, puts in a central line stating his pain ("to see you has been enough anguish"), and then repeats the conditional idea in the next three lines. This 3-1-3 pattern is followed by the closing *mudanza* and *retornelo,* which logically question what there would be to see if she were not to be seen. The song thus closes with the same linguistic pattern as it began: "si," "no," "os," "hubiera mirado-mirara," forming thereby a circular structure from which, because of the nature of courtly love, the poet cannot or desires not to escape.

Finally, the poem is characteristic of courtly poetry in that it has no nouns. In place of the substantives, which would give the *villancico* the earthly, descriptive concreteness all lovers attempt to overcome, there are thirteen verbal forms. The poem thus breaks away entirely from the world of things, *les mots et les choses,* to penetrate into the realm of the abstract spiritual universe of feeling. The bard's entire universe of being has become sublimated to the desire to see his lady and to suffer the pangs of amour. There is no hint of wanting anything more or of being concerned with anything else; nor is there any notion that the poet wishes to utilize this burning passion to purify his soul so as to soar to a higher realm of being, as the later Platonic doctrines will require. On the contrary, he voluntarily allows his being to be ensnared in the negative paradox of *not* wanting anything but to see his mistress.

Boscán's love for his lady, which is the one and only theme of all the poetry in Book One, is thus a physical passion characterized by suffering, pain, anguish, unfulfilled desire, and constant longing to be with the beloved. His Castilian poetry is, in sum, totally courtly; and it contains all the characteristics of that style. The precise sources that Boscán drew upon for inspiration in composing this type of poetry are impossible to determine, since almost everyone was employing the same style; but the major influences are from the Spanish *Cancionero* tradition, the Catalan Ausias March (1397–1459), and the Italian bard Francesco Petrarca (1304–1374).[4] The first influence gave Boscán meters and content; March lent the poet a melancholic tone and the abstract, almost scholastic, manner of analyzing the state of a desperately sad soul; while Petrarch infused Boscán's poetry with a spiritual tone that was new to Span-

ish poetry[5] and that increases in Boscán's writings when the Italian
meters are adopted. The unique blend of these diverse currents is
what separates Boscán's poesy from the mass of similar writings by
his contemporaries, and it is what marks him as a man of the
Renaissance.

II Castilian Canciones

The six *canciones* in Spanish meters are written in octosyllables
of from twelve to fifteen lines. They are all courtly in theme. The
first four concern the paradox of a love that kills but which gives
life to the lover, and the last two treat the departure of the mistress
from the lover's presence. *Canción* I is the most exemplificative of
Boscán's early style. It also follows closely the techniques utilized
in his *villancico;* and, as the name implies, it, too, was meant to be
sung to the accompaniment of music. The song has twelve lines and
rhymes abbacddcabba.

Canción I

¿Qué haré? que por quereros
mis estremos son tan claros,
que ni soy para miraros,
ni puedo dexar de veros.
Yo no sé con vuestra ausencia
un punto vivir ausente,
ni puedo sufrir presente,
Señora, tan gran presencia;
de suerte que por quereros
mis estremos son tan claros,
que ni soy para miraros,
ni puedo dexar de veros.   (p. 128)

(What will I do? for by desiring you
my sufferings are so obvious,
that I am not capable of seeing you,
nor can I stop seeing you.
I do not know how, when you are absent,
to live an instant absent from you,
nor can I suffer when you are present,
Lady, such a great presence;
so that for desiring you
my sufferings are so obvious,

that I am not capable of seeing you,
nor can I stop seeing you.)

This *canción,* like the *villancico,* is based entirely on verbal forms, with the important exceptions of "extremos," "ausencia," and "presencia." It is the latter two nouns, of course, which cause the first. The *canción* expresses the negative paradox of courtly love in even a more inescapable manner than did the *villancico,* for here the paradox offers no alternatives to A: I cannot do A, nor can I do not-A. This negativity again forces the poet into a spiritual cul-de-sac, since now he cannot live seeing her nor not seeing her. The circularity of the song thus becomes absolute, for the poet finds himself subjected entirely to a circumstance which paralyzes his existence. Boscán also structures his twelve-line pattern even more closed than the scheme of the *villancico* by reusing the first four lines for the last four. This repetition (which lends a sense of timelessness to the poem, since one assumes that the pattern is infinite) sandwiches the middle four lines and their central idea. The poet further emphasizes the circular inescapability of his poem by structuring the nouns of the central quartet in a circular pattern of "ausencia"-"ausente"-"presente"-"presencia" (n-adj-adj-n), and by creating parallel lines of the two center verses:

un pun-to vi-vir au-sen-te
ni pue-do su-frir pre-sen-te

The canción thus closes in upon itself on all sides, precisely as the poet's dilemma entraps him in a paradoxical snare from which it is impossible to escape. The structural circularity thus reflects a semantic circularity which reflects the poet's spiritual existence.

III *Coplas*

The most important pieces in Book One are the *coplas.* The term *copla* refers to any poem with eight-syllable lines and consonantal rhyme.[6] There is thus a wide variety of rhyme forms and stanza lengths in Boscán's *coplas.* The 1543 princeps edition contained nineteen poems, which were expanded in later printings to thirty-one, and finally to thirty-eight in the 1875 Knapp edition. The original group of nineteen is of central concern, because only these

can be considered with assurance to have been ordered by Boscán,
along with the six *canciones,* into a sequence. He could have
received the idea of writing the history of his loves in a group of
independent poems from any number of medieval poets, including
Ausias March. The most famous example is of course Petrarch's
sequence to Laura entitled *Il Canzoniere,* where in the first sonnet
he declares he is going to present "rime sparse" that will outline
his love affair.[7] Moreover, *Coplas* I–XVIII are different from the
others in that they are all courtly love songs. *Coplas* XIX–XXXI (in
the Knapp edition) are epistolary poems between Boscán and
other men about the effects of love, and *Coplas* XXXII–XXXVIII
are various short pieces that do not really fall into any group.

The original sequence has been admirably described by J.P.
Wickersham Crawford.[8] He notes that *Coplas* I–VIII describe the
course of Juan Boscán's passion for one Doña Isabel, whom the
poet names in *Copla* II. His sufferings begin the moment he sees
her (*Copla* I), when he realizes that love is bittersweet (II). A mis-
understanding has parted them and he wishes he had never seen the
lady (III). He nevertheless regrets the lovers' quarrel that precipitated it (IV), and remains disconsolate (V). He now determines to
cure his lover's malady by departing from his lady's presence, as
one has an injured finger amputated in order to save the hand (VI).
He speaks of his sadness (VII); but he feels free, although his soul
still lives in his lady's heart (VIII). He compares his bifurcated situation to the phoenix, the fountains which are hot and cold and bring
laughter and sadness, the basilisk, and the eagle (IX), images which
Boscán may have borrowed from Petrarch's *Canzone* number 135
("Qual più diversa e nova") in *Il Canzoniere.* If Petrarch is indeed
the direct source, it would imply either that Boscán knew the bard's
poetry before he took up the Italian meters in 1526 or that Boscán
composed *Copla* IX after experimenting with the new forms. The
former hypothesis seems the more likely, since Boscán told the
Duchess of Somma in his letter that after 1526 he abandoned Castilian meters entirely. M. Menéndez Pelayo (pp. 224–27) is of this
same opinion. The *copla* sequence continues with Boscán sur-
rendering to his lady's wishes (X), and lamenting that he is dying
because she will not pardon him (XI); but he finally frees his will
from his mistress's grasp and declares himself no longer her captive
(XII).

The remainder of the *coplas,* according to Crawford, treat a second round of adventures: "*Coplas* XIII–XXV reflect another love affair, which the poet takes care to place upon a higher plane. Once again he runs love's gamut, passing from mere gallantry to desire, jealousy (XV), the conflict between hope and fear, with an occasional cry of triumph" (p. 31). Specifically, *Copla* XIII presents the positive side (there are no negatives) of the courtly liaison, where the lover praises his good fortune for having fallen in love with the lady; but in the following *copla* Boscán expresses his love in terms of imprisonment of the will, and begs his mistress to reciprocate. In *Copla* XV his love has degenerated into jealousy, which drives the poet to the zenith of his sufferings and even to the contemplation of death. His pain is further augmented by the fact that this is the second time he has fallen in love. After an interlude (XVI) in which Boscán sends to a friend some of his love poetry, the poet turns on his mistress and accuses her of allowing another courtier to serve her in his absence (XVII); but his fierce love is not abated (XVIII), and he finds himself visiting the places where his lady will appear. The last *copla* in the series is an epistle from Boscán to Admiral Fadrique Enríquez (died 1538), in which the poet rejects all past loves for the present one.

As the reader can see from this brief description, the second affair is not really on a higher plane; if anything, it is more intense and entails more pain and suffering. The major difference is that the second love is more discursive, as can be seen in the greater length of the *coplas* in this second group. This digressiveness gives a tone of higher rationality on the poet's part because the compactness and tenseness of the short poem is lost. The second group of *coplas* is also more social. Boscán speaks of rivals, friends, enemies; one (XIII) is a gloss of a poem by Jorge Manrique and two (XVI and XX) are directed to other people. These characteristics make the songs appear to describe a higher level of love, although such is not the case. All the *coplas,* in effect, are typical courtly love poems similar to the popular verses published in the *cancioneros* contemporary with Boscán. One can conclude without much dispute, therefore, that all the pieces in this original sequence were composed before 1526, when Boscán began to write in Italian meters, and obviously before 1533, when he translated the Platonically oriented *Il cortegiano* of Baldassar Castiglione.

It goes without saying that Boscán retouched and perhaps even rewrote the *coplas* before their publication in 1543, as any con-

scientious writer would do; but he probably left the sense and tone
of the verses intact. A comparison of *Copla* XV as it was published
in the princeps edition with an earlier broadside printing, discovered by Hayward Keniston and known as *Las treinta,* indicates
clearly in the numerous variants between the two printed specimens
that Boscán altered words and even lines at will, although the
meaning and sensibility of the pieces remained intact.[9] Furthermore, it is patent that he selected these particular pieces for artistic
reasons. He must have thought them either the best or the most
representative of his poems, and he must have wanted them to be
read in a particular sequence. The twelve additional *coplas* that
appeared in the Antwerp, 1534, edition were most likely poems that
Boscán had set aside to be published but had excluded from the
original group because they did not fit well into the sequence. The
haphazard order and the subject matter of those last twelve *coplas*
justify this hypothesis.

     Another logistic problem not taken into account by Crawford is
that the six *canciones* are intermixed with the nineteen *coplas* in the
original version of Boscán's works. *Canción* I is after *Copla* II;
Canciones II and III are together after *Copla* V; *Canciones* IV and
V are together after *Villancico* II, which follows *Copla* XVI; and
Cancion VI comes before the last *copla,* which is addressed "Al
Almirante de Castilla." By intertwining different types of poems in
this way, Boscán was following the example of Petrarch in *Il
Canzoniere,* who interspersed his *canzoni* among the sonnets to
form his sequence. Luckily, Boscán's inclusion of the *canciones*
among the *coplas* is in no way deleterious to Crawford's description of the events described in the sequence, for the subject matter
of the *canciones* fits in quite well with that of the *coplas.*

     The first *copla* is typical in form and content of all the poems in
the original sequence. It has eight stanzas of ten octosyllabic lines
except that lines 2, 6 and 8 have *pie quebrado.* The rhyme scheme is
aabbaccddc, with a sharp break after the fifth line.[10] The first
stanza reads:

Copla I

1.   Siento mi congoxa tal
       que mi mal,
       aunque es malo de sentirse,
       es tan bueno de sufrirse

que no puede ser mortal;
es tan fuerte
que bien puede dar muerte:
mas la vida
va muy lexos de perdida,
pues gana la mejor parte.　　(p. 15)

(I feel my complaint in such a way
that my illness,
although it hurts to feel it,
is so good to suffer it
that it cannot be mortal;
it is so strong
that it can easily bring death:
but my life goes a long way from being lost,
since it wins the best fate.)

The subject matter of the stanza is characteristic of courtly love poetry. The poet suffers incredible pain, but enjoys the torments because they are the barometer that measures his love. He plays on the words "malo" and "bueno," "mal" and "bien," by saying that his sickness ("mal") is good ("bueno"), and by rhyming internally "mal" in line 2 with "malo" in line 3; for they both have the third syllable line stress. "Bueno" in the next line also has this emphasis, which adds to the paradoxical quality of the expression; and the first quintet is rounded off by placing the same stress on a word that rhymes vocally with "bueno:" "que no *pue*de ser mortal." The same interplay of internal rhymes and opposites is seen in the second quintet, where "*fue*rte" and "*pue*de" form a vocal relationship, and the end word "muerte" is followed by its opposite, "vida." The poet thus creates the ultimate courtly paradox by saying that "fuerte muerte" and "vida perdida" bring "suerte."

This idea that the greatest suffering is pleasure and that all the things that appear to be bad luck are good luck is what unifies the thought of the poem. In the second stanza Boscán notes how everyone warns that his fantasy is working against him; but he responds that, although such is the case, he enjoys it that way because it leaves him more satisfied. The third stanza is a blatant exaltation of the tormented flesh:

3.   Mi alma se favorece
     si padece,
     y toma por mejoría
     que crezca la pena mía;
     mas a ratos mucho crece.
     Yo la siento,
     mas della no me arrepiento,
     que el amor,
     a medida del dolor,
     suele dar el sufrimiento.   (p. 16)

     (My soul is favored if it suffers,
     and considers as a recuperation
     that my pain should increase;
     but at times it increases too much.
     I feel it,
     but I do not repent of it,
     for love,
     equal with the pain,
     usually brings suffering.)

Here there is no paradox, but the simple statement that love is suffering, so therefore his soul considers pain to be a desirable part of being in love. The form of the stanza is admirably knit by the repetition of the *m* sound (mi, ma, ma, me, mí, ma, mu, ma, me, mo, me, mi). The last two lines, which carry the conceptual equalization of love and suffering, close the stanza with a series of *d* sounds (di, da, de, do) in line 9 and a symmetrical final line with *su, da* (to rhyme internally with the earlier line), *su*.

The following stanzas describe how the poet came to find himself in this paradoxical predicament. Boscán makes the point that it is only he who suffers this way, and not his beloved; then he explains how quickly he fell in love and how he now serves her, although he does not understand her. Nevertheless, this lack of comprehension does not bother him too much because, as he says in the final lines, he loves her with his will, not with his understanding. The poet thus closes the verses with the inevitable declaration of the courtier that love is an act of the blind will in which reason has no part: "Sobrarme la voluntad,/ do falta el entendimiento" (p. 17). Boscán will not recognize the role of reason in love until Sonnet LXXVII in Book Two, when he incorporates the ideas of the Florentine Academy into his poetry.

Another appealing *copla* is number VIII. It is a short piece of twenty-two octosyllabic lines in two stanzas, rhyming abcabcddeed, with a sharp break after the sixth line:

Copla VIII

1. Señora, libre me siento:
    mi querer tras vos le envío:
    suelta va mi voluntad,
    que pues en mi mal consiento,
    no forzando el albedrío,
    no pierdo mi libertad.
    No la pierdo en algun hora
    mi alma, pues en vos mora:
    que ved si es ancha prisión
    vivir en el corazón
    de vuestra merced, Señora.

2. Allá estoy: ¿no me sentis?
    ni es mucho en tan gran morada
    tal huésped que no se sienta:
    no me cerráis, ni me abrís.
    ¿Qué hará el alma cuitada
    perdida con tal afrenta?
    Uno soy, y en uno dos,
    hay un ser solo entre nos,
    con que yo muy claro muestro
    que imposible es no ser vuestro,
    siendo vos, Señora, vos.   (p. 31)

    (Lady, I feel myself free:
I send my desire after you:
my will goes freed,
for since I give consent to my ill,
not forcing my will,
I do not lose my freedom.
My soul does not miss it at any time,
since it also lives in you:
so you shall see if it is a large prison
to live in the heart
of your ladyship, Lady.

    There I am: do you not feel me?
It is strange that in such a large mansion

such a great guest should not be felt:
you do not close me in nor do you open up for me.
What will the anxious soul do
lost with such an affront?
I am one, and one in two,
there is only one being between us,
with which I show very clearly,
that it is impossible not to be yours,
being you, Lady, you.)

This is Boscán's only poem with eleven lines, and he uses it excellently by putting the central idea of each stanza in the sixth line. The same technique is used in *Copla* V, which has seven-line stanzas, and in *Copla* VII, which has nine-line stanzas. There, the fourth and fifth lines respectively carry the central statements.

As seen, *Copla* VIII, like most of Boscán's better verses, exhibits a good circular balance. The first line presents the apostrophe to his lady, and the last lines of both stanzas end with the same reference. Moreover, the first line has a symmetry formed by "*señora...siento*," and the final line has a similar one formed by "*siendo — vos señora — vos*." Other admirable poetic techniques are the use of the negative way so characteristic of courtly poetry (*no* appears eight times), bifurcation in lines 1, 4, 7, and 11 of the second stanza, and polyptoton in the use of *ser* in the second part of the same stanza ("*soy*," "*un ser*," "*ser*," "*siendo*"). The main interest of the poem, however, is in the ingenuity of the idea that the poet's will is free because he has freely given it to his lady, and yet the will is still attached to his soul because it too inhabits her heart. Boscán complains that his lady does not recognize this new resident within her; but, by way of the verbal interplay of one-in-two, he points out to her that they are now one entity while and, paradoxically, because she remains who she is. The absence of the traditional vocabulary of sickness, suffering, torments, and complaints gives this *copla* a lighter touch than the others, and thereby elevates it to a higher degree of finesse and poetic sensibility. Its very brevity, moreover, gives it a certain cohesiveness that will not be equaled until Boscán begins to work with the sonnet format.

IV *"Conversión de Boscán"*

The "Conversión de Boscán" (for a translation and the original

Spanish see Appendix C) appeared in the Antwerp, 1544, edition of the poet's works at the end of the *copla* sequence; and it rightly deserves a place there, for it is a proper colophon to the courtly love process. Like all courtly bards, Boscán closed the amorous period of his youth with an apparently sincere palinode denouncing his past folly.[11] It presents, moreover, a kind of sequence, for in it Boscán describes the process of his love from the basest elements to the heights of understanding, following precisely the Aristotelian-Thomistic theories of the soul.

According to traditional theory, the universe consisted of the four elements or "calidades": earth, water, air, and fire. They were, respectively, cold and dry, cold and wet, hot and wet, and hot and dry. The humors, melancholy, phlegm, blood, and choler, were fabricated in the body by a predominance of one of these elements. Likewise, there were thought to be three souls, a vegetative, a sensitive, and a rational soul.[12] To the first belonged all the natural world of minerals, plants, and waters. The second soul appeared in the animals and was what gave them movement and procreation. The rational soul was found only in man and was what separated him from the rest of creation and gave him his angelic nature. Moreover, as the animals also had a vegetative soul, so man had all three souls within himself; and he was supposed to subordinate the lower two through the proper use of the rational soul and his divinely endowed will.

Included in the traditional beliefs about the faculty psychology of man was the composition of the intellect, where rational ideas are formed. The object in nature entered through the eyes or one or more of the other senses and was presented to the common sense for reconstruction as a coherent image. It then passed through the imaginative faculty, the sensitive memory, the fantasy, and the estimative faculty. From there, having been transformed into a phantasm, it went to the upper part of the brain to be converted into an idea of the object by the mind. The image was then presented to the three highest powers of the soul, the understanding ("entendimiento"), memory ("memoria"), and will ("voluntad").[13] The understanding decided if the object was good or bad and, if it considered it worthy, presented it to the memory for safekeeping. The will, which was considered to be blind, put the idea into action when it was taken from the memory. There also existed in the human system many passions, generally separated into irascible

and concupiscible appetites. These were rightly relegated to the
sensitive soul; but they were so powerful that, if the reason suc-
cumbed to them, they could dictate to the will actions that were
deleterious to the human condition.

Boscán uses these well-known theories as the structural format
for the spiritual pilgrimage of the soul he describes in "Boscán's
Conversion." The poem is written in the meter termed *copla real*.[14]
Each stanza has ten octosyllabic lines rhyming either abbabcdcdc
or abbabcddcc or ababacdcdc or ababacedcd. There are thirty-five
stanzas. The work has two equal parts, both written in the preterite
tense, establishing thereby the retrospective tone. The first part
describes Boscán's descent into spiritual captivity, and the second
half describes his ascent and liberation.

The poem (see Appendix C for the text and translation) opens
with the bard's discovery that his soul is in mortal danger because
after so many disillusionments he finds that he has yet to fulfill the
timeless dictate *gnothi seauton* ("know thyself"). The emphasis is
on the verbs "ver" and "conocer," which are the two things the
poet has neglected to do; and he juxtaposes "suelo" and "cielo" to
show the reader where he is and to where he wishes to go. He recognizes his sickness as the absence of control over the major potencies
of his soul, the will, which is without rein, and the understanding,
which is tied to the senses. His soul is therefore metaphorically
dead, because it is buried in the body. His rational faculties ("mi
seso") are completely reversed; and, because his immortal spirit is
bound by his mortal desires, his whole nature is upside down. The
emphasis in the third, fourth, and fifth stanzas is still on sight
("ver" is used fourteen times in the first fifty lines). His rational
soul, that which makes man Godlike, is in a state of decay; he has
embraced the bad and has neglected the good; and his fantasy
reigns in his mind. The first four stanzas are thus permeated with
the antithesis of where Boscán is and where he should be: "suelo"-
"cielo," "no conocerme"-"conocerme," "cuerpo"-"alma,"
"muerte"-"vivo," "pies"-"cabeza," "mortal"-"inmortal,"
"flaco"-"esfuerzo," "siniestra"-"diestra," "malo"-"bueno."

The four elements, which are naturally so contrary, have consented to the basest desires, and what he thought was victory has
been defeat. What is worse, Boscán admits that he became accustomed to living in such a state and fled the occasions when reason
tried to illuminate his darkened soul. He lowered himself to the

lowest elements — the vegetative state — and dragged his judgment down with him. His blindness turned him into a base animal ("alimaña") in which the being with which he was born was lost and he failed to recognize his own self. He desired to regenerate his spirit, however, and enlisted the aid of a friend, whom the reader only knows as "aquél"; but the friend left him helpless after the initial offer of aid. Boscán, describing his state as that of a child learning to walk, attempted again to wrest his spirit from degeneracy, and arrived at the first plateau, where grace could begin to be achieved.

The next four stanzas (14-17) present Boscán's regeneration in terms of the sun dawning slowly but surely after a dark night. The metaphor, which forms the thread for all four stanzas, is a brilliantly devised way to describe the painful, uncertain process of forcing the will to respond to right reason. Boscán describes how the light — ancient symbol of rationality and self-awareness — began to break through the darkness; and, although the sun did not yet appear, patches of blue could be seen. Observing that it was indeed the dawning of a new life, the poet gathered strength and began to order his life and to awaken from the dreamlike state he was in. Comparing his situation to the shepherd who awakens on a chilly morning in his cabin and arises chilled to walk along the mountain, blowing on his cold hands and shaking himself, so his soul, deadened by so many vain desires, thus found itself at last alive. Boscán saw in the now-serene air the abyss into which he had fallen, and recognized how much he had not known his own self. Finally, he perceived the sun in all its clear beauty; and, although it was still in the east, there was enough light to see the goal he must reach. In stanza eighteen, the center of the poem, he received help a second time, and he was able to walk along the proper path, cured of his spiritual illness.

The first half of "Boscán's Conversion" thus delineates the fall of the poet into a spiritual death and his arduous struggle to bring his rational soul back to life. He describes the descent as a disordering of his senses and a binding of his higher faculties by the appetites. The return is compared to the dawning of a new day after a dark and stormy night. In the second part of the poem, Boscán, now sane and whole, looks inward into his self rather than backward to his past. The verb "ver" thus again dominates the verses (it begins eight of the last seventeen stanzas), but now in a spatial sense rather than in a temporal one. First the bard looked back into time and presented a history of his love illness; now the trajectory vectors into inner space so the poet can describe the composition of his regenerated soul.

Well-reminded of how asleep he was, striving for the summit, and aware of the evils that he left behind, Boscán turned to his soul, witnessed the inner man ("mi hombre que está dentro"), and set about converting him to his original state. He perceived the interior kingdom in proper order, with reason in control. The three souls were all functioning properly, with the rational one commanding and the other two obeying. He saw next his fantasy, who like a naughty child wanted to be mischievous; but his reason would not allow it. His base passions were also there, but they showed little signs of life. Boscán then saw the highest part of his rational soul, where his understanding ruled the will; and he espied the memory, which contained his long history and reminded him continually of his errors so that now he could correct his present state. The memory, in effect, put his past and his future before him; and his sorrow at his faults freed him from them.

Finally, Boscán progressed further within his soul and thought upon his Creator. He saw that God redeemed him, being cruel to Himself, and became man so that man could become God ("vi como se hizo él yo, / porque yo me hiciese él"). The poet comprehended that when God created him He gave him free will to make the choice to become bestial, merely human, or angelical. He understood that God was providential in every act, and that He created Hell solely to warn man that if he could avoid it he would gain Paradise; and he inferred that God's justice was always merciful. Seeing these things within his soul, Boscán heartily repented and converted his life to God. He then felt his soul lifted to the highest level, and found peace in death of the flesh, that same flesh that at the beginning of the poem had caused the death of his spirit. With the highest grace that comes with this moral state, Boscán found that at last virtue had become his natural self. Blind now to the world's ills, as he had earlier been blind to the world's goods, the poet encounters that pure consonance in which inconstancy ceases to exist.

Thus runs the argument of Boscán's most moving and most personal poem. It is in relation to this first Book of courtly poems — which describe the imprisonment of the will by love and the absolute sublimation of the flesh in unattainable desire — in the same proportion as the "Epistle to Mendoza" will be in relation to the Italianate poetry — where love will eventually become an exercise in spiritual illumination. Sonnet XC and *Canción* X, which are also palinodes, will describe a middle ground between these two longer confessions. As the "Conversion" terminates with the mortification of the flesh ("que la carne estuvo muerta / de quedar el alma viva"), that flesh in which the courtier glorified when unretributed desire burned in his soul, so the "Epistle to Mendoza" will end with sexual fulfillment of the flesh in a happy marriage of two harmonious souls. Clearly, given the nature of the love described in the *coplas,* Boscán's conversion could only be one of mortification and repentance for a kind of love that was considered a mortal sin. He, as all medieval lovers, thus returned to the arms of Mother Church when he tired of the dance of love.

V *"Mar de amor" and "Ospital de amor"*

Another poem that appeared in the Antwerp, 1544, edition but was not in the princeps is the "Sea of Love." It is a long excursis of five hundred ten lines in ten-line *coplas reales* on Boscán's dangerous navigation through the Sea of Love, all for the sake of suffering greater pain for the glory of his lady. The tone and sense of the poem are thus the same as in his *coplas.* He defines love as a "fuerza del alma," then borrows a traditional emblem of Friendship to describe love's appearance:

Mar de amor

4.　　Es verde su vestidura
　　　con que ceba al inocente,
　　　lexos y cerca, en la frente,
　　　es su señal y pintura,
　　　porque ama el que es ausente.
　　　Trae abierto el corazon
　　　y allí escrito con la mano:
　　　muerte y vida en conclusión;
　　　y en el pecho otro renglón
　　　que dice: invierno y verano (p. 1

　　　(Its dress is green
　　　with which it baits the innocent soul,
　　　"far and near" on its forehead

> is the sign and painting,
> because it loves what is absent.
> It has its chest exposed
> and there written with the hand:
> "death and life" in the end;
> and on its bosom another line
> that says: "Winter and Summer.")

The poet is captured by this love and sees only death as a way of escape, but he also realizes that the escape would bring death, for he is now like a fish who cannot live out of the sea. So he slowly feeds his pain to sustain it and continues to toil at serving his lady: "el oficio de servir" (p. 149). Boscán then repeats the traditional topics of courtly love: "verme muriendo vivir; / y si vivo en mi morir" (p. 151). He compares his state to the condition of certain animals — the cat, the crocodile, the deer, the monkey, and the eagle — and he terminates by again stressing the paradoxicalness of his floundering in the sea of passion. There he will certainly drown if he stays, but he will suffocate like a fish out of water if he leaves; so he decides that he must remain in this sea to fulfill his one reason for existence.

In "Mar de amor" there is thus little difference from any of the other Castilian verses, except for the length. It is representative in every way of the pre-conversion period, and was assuredly put after the "Conversión de Boscán" rather than before simply because it was the longest of the poet's early verses.

A similar traditional piece by Juan Boscán is the "Hospital of Love," a poem of six hundred and thirty lines, only in manuscript form.[15] The work has ten-line octasyllable strophes rhyming ababacdcdc. Its most immediate source is an "Hôpital d'Amour" by Achille Caulier (before 1441). The "Hospital of Love" is in the *amorosa visione* tradition in that the events described therein are all part of the world of dreams. The poem begins with Boscán awaking one night because of the pain and torment he is suffering from raging love. He is visited by a comely damsel dressed in dark green. She informs the poet that she used to be his friend, but now he has cast her aside. She is of course Hope *(Esperanza)* and she undertakes to carry her lovesick charge on a cloud to a lonely field, where he meets a hermit. Boscán tells the hermit he is a hopeless prisoner of love; and the man, who is Care *(Cuidado),* leads the bard to his hospital. Over the entrance of the sanatorium is an image of Cupid controlling the stars and planets. There is another image of many lovers with Fortune over them. Boscán describes many of the residents of the hospital as he is guided by an old man who is the physician. The doctor prescribes cures in learned medical terms that all entail psychological acts of the will by the inflicted lovers, such as putting one's mind on other things, knowing oneself, having patience and fortitude, and exerting one's reason. Boscán then describes to the physician his love symptoms, but Boscán's wounds are so old and so deep that he is beyond cure, so they put him into a bed to die. The physician counsels Boscán to inform his lady of his ills by way of a sound-minded person called Thought *(Pensamiento)*, who comes often to pray for the sick. Boscán follows the doctor's advice and sends Thought with a supplication to his lady. The poem ends at this point.

The tone and style of "Ospital de amor" place it clearly in the same artistic period as the "Mar de amor." Both poems delight in detailing the torments and sufferings of noble love. Both are also conceptualistic in that they select a central theme (the sea and a hospital) to play on the terminology in terms of courtly love. This kind of "medieval" wittiness will disappear completely in the next Book of "Renaissance" sonnets and *canciones*.

CHAPTER 3

The Second Book: Italianate Poetry

I *Sonnets*

BOOK Two of Juan Boscán's poetry contains ten Italianate *canciones* and ninety-two sonnets, although not in that order. The last two sonnets are epitaphs to Garcilaso de la Vega; the other poems form a sequence in which the poet describes his courtly love affairs and his conversion to the new Platonic love delineated by the Italian Neoplatonic philosophers and poets.

According to J. P. Wickersham Crawford, the sonnet sequence can be divided into two parts: Sonnets I–XXV and Sonnets XXVI–XC. The first group is analogous to *Coplas* I–XII, while the second group reflects the love affair described in *Coplas* XIII–XXV. Referring to Sonnets I–XXV, Crawford states:

The first four of these serve as an introduction to the sequence, and he explains that he displays his wounds so that others may be deterred from following in his footsteps. Doomed to unhappy love from his cradle (V), he foresees no change in his sad fate (VI); alone and dispirited he seeks out deserted places (VII); he wished to love his lady discreetly (*blandamente*), but with this she was not satisfied (VIII); he has lost faith in pleasure (IX); he suffers the pangs of disillusion (X) and prefers death to his present anguish (XI); he regrets his old love, but cannot be happy (XII); as new torments assail him, he shudders at the past and longs for death (XIII–XV), yet he yearns to see the eyes that cause his pain, separated from him by so many plains and mountains (XVI); but doubts still torment him and the fire of love still smoulders (XVIII–XXV). ("Chronology," pp. 29–30)

"The course of his new love," continues Crawford, "is described also in his Sonnets XXVIII–XC. New hopes fill the heart (XXVII), but he is timid and distrusts love (XXVIII–XXXII); he cannot understand why he should seek again the cause of his ills (XXXVII); his desires are renewed as the trees and flowers spring into new life (XXXVIII).... He now directs himself more openly to the lady, picturing to her his distress in a series of sonnets until we reach the exultant cry of the seventy-seventh.... We may assume that by this time he has been accepted as a lover, or rather as a husband, for in the closing sonnets he insists that the love he now feels is pure, and that he was cured of his moral paralysis by 'the chaste love that God sends from heaven' '' (p. 33). Later in the study (p. 35), Crawford subdivides this last category into Sonnets XXVIII–LXXVI, which parallel the events in *Coplas* XIII–XXV, and Sonnets LXXVII–XC, which forecast Boscán's marriage to Doña Ana Girón de Rebolledo.

There are numerous caveats in a disposition of this nature. In the first place, a parallelization of the subject matter in the *coplas* and in the sonnets would mean that Boscán wrote them concurrently, thus negating the theory that all the Spanish meters were written before all the Italianate meters. Assuredly, some of the *coplas* were composed or at least rewritten after 1526; but in his preface to Book Two directed to the Duchess of Somma (see Appendix A), Boscán states categorically that when he undertook to write in Italian meters he abandoned forever the old style. In the second place, Crawford's divisions imply that the sonnet sequence, as well as the *copla* sequence, was written cumulatively by Boscán; in other words, the sonnets which appear first were written first. This hypothesis is difficult to accept. The first four introductory sonnets were probably written last and then placed in their present position; and although Sonnets V–LXXVI do indeed present a "historia de mis males" (Sonnet II), a "curso desta historia" (Sonnet LXXXVI), they are of such a homogeneous nature that it would be imprecise to equate their present order to chronological order of composition. The only supposition that helps Crawford's biographical disposition of the sonnets is that, although Boscán did not write the first seventy-six sonnets in their present order, the poet assuredly put them in that order so as to create a logical sequence of events in the life of a typical lover.

Another thing that Crawford failed to take into account was the intercalation of the Italianate *canciones* with the sonnets. *Canciones* I and II follow Sonnet XVIII, *Canciones* III and IV follow

Sonnet XXI, *Canción* V follows Sonnet XXXIII, *Canción* VI follows Sonnet XL, *Canción* VII follows LXII, and *Canciones* VIII
and IX follow Sonnet LXVII. The last *canción,* which is a courtly
palinode, rightly comes at the end of Book Two.

One thing is certain. All the sonnets before Sonnet LXXVII (with
the exception of the four introductory ones but including all nine
intercalated *canciones*) were written before the last fourteen poems.
As will be shown, Sonnets LXXVII–XC present a radical change in
tone, style, language, and content from the earlier ones. It is as if in
Sonnet LXXVII Boscán suddenly "discovered" Platonic love and
immediately rejected Aristotelian love. Crawford believed that the
new tone and language was brought about by Boscán's marrying,
or at least falling in love with, Ana Girón. Yet it is difficult to believe that a change in Boscán's personal feelings could bring about
so profound a change in tone, style, language, and poetic structure.
Rather than ascribing the metamorphosis to an alteration of feelings, it is more logical to attribute it to exposure to a new poetic
method of describing one's personal emotions. In other words, the
feelings did not change; the artistic manner of expressing them did;
and the motivation for the conversion was assuredly Boscán's
absorption of the philosophy in Book IV of Baltassare
Castiglione's *Il cortegiano* in 1533, along with his inevitable exposure to the other material by the Florentine Neoplatonists.

M. Menéndez Pelayo also noted the enormous change in
Boscán's sensibilities that took place within the sonnet sequence.
He attributed it to the natural elegance of the hendecasyllable,
which allowed Boscán to say things he was unable to express in the
shorter Castilian verses: "Boscán was not only an innovator in
metrical forms, but in the intimate and substantial forms of the
poetry. In his sonnets and in his *canciones* love is taken seriously,
and although it still appears metaphysical and vague to us, it has
from time to time accents of sincerity that do not deceive. Only by
writing in hendecasyllables does Boscán reach a certain level of
poetic emotion, intermingled at times with gracious realistic details.
Nothing or almost nothing of this is in his short verses, although
they may be more correct in language and rhythm."[1] Menéndez
Pelayo was clearly just as mistaken to state that solely a change in
verse form can bring about a change in expression as was Crawford
to believe that a change in personal feelings alone could bring about
the new sensibilities. Assuredly, both the new meter and the new

affair played a decisive role; but the requisite without which the new poetic sensibility would never have occurred was decidedly the new kind of love that Boscán felt. For proof are sonnets I–LXXVI and the *canciones,* which use the new meters to express the old love, and the fact that surely few poets underwent such a radical shift in thought and sensitivity when they got married.

In sum, the sequence can be divided logically into two parts. Sonnets I–LXXVI (plus *Canciones* I–IX) describe Boscán's courtly loves and were conceivably written between 1526–1533; Sonnets LXXVII–XC present Boscán's acceptance of the Platonic system of love and were probably written after 1533. The first group, moreover, may also refer to a love before 1526 that the poet describes retrospectively in the first twenty-five sonnets; this would account for the light break in the sequence between Sonnets XXV and XXVIII.

As is well known, the sonnet is a fourteen line poem in hendeca-syllables with four parts: two quartets and two tercets. In Boscán's poetry, the quartets always rhyme abba,abba; but the tercets vary considerably. Cdc,dcd is the most predominant, occurring twenty-seven times, followed by cdc,cdc (twenty-five poems), cde,cde (in nineteen sonnets), and cde,dce (in twenty sonnets).[2] The central stress in Boscán's verses typically falls on the sixth syllable, and the most common accentuation is on syllables 2, 6, 10, as in "buscándo el amór contentamiénto." This is normally referred to as a heroic line. If the first of the accents is on the initial syllable, it is called an emphatic line; if on the third syllable, a melodic line; and if on the fourth syllable, a Sapphic line. Boscán uses all four types through-out his sonnet sequence. Another characteristic of Boscán's sonnets is the rare use of *versos agudos,* or verses in which the accent falls on the last syllable, forming a breath syllable at the end, as, for example, in Sonnet XVI: "y volver mal, sin esperar sazón." *Versos agudos,* which abound in Boscán's Castilian poetry, are used solely in Sonnets XVI, XX, XLI, XLII, LI, and LXXVII. The absence of this type of verse is characteristic of the poet's hendecasyllable. In "Leandro y Hero," written in blank verse, there is only one line that employs it ("lo que es y lo que fue y lo que será"); "Capítulo I," composed in *terza rima,* has none at all, and the "Octava rima," in royal octaves, has only four or five. Not surprisingly, Boscán never uses the *verso esdrújulo,* where there are two unac-cented syllables after the final stress.

The first four sonnets form a long paragraph in which Boscán
explains that he is publishing in his poetry "la historia de mis
males" (Sonnet II) so that others will be undeceived before they fall
into the same sad state as he did. In Sonnet I he says that he never
thought he would find himself writing verses in praise of love, but
he hopes his verse will serve as a caveat to those who take pleasure
in reading about others' torments ("gustando de leer tormentos
tristes"). The wounds left by love are still visible, he explains in
Sonnet II, and he is ashamed to show them in public; i.e., he is
ashamed to expose his inner sufferings by publishing his works.
Sonnet III follows the idea of the preceding one by beginning with
"But:" "Mas mientras más yo desto me corriere." Although it
bothers him to expose his misadventures, he feels obligated to do so
for the well-being of others. Finally, in Sonnet IV, he asks who
could be so insensitive as not to turn from love after seeing the
effects it has had on him.

These first sonnets are thus written in retrospect after the poet
has suffered the agonies that will appear in the rest of the poems.
From Sonnet II, moreover, the reader knows that the composer is
now cured of his love sickness and is publishing his verses only out
of compassion for others who may fall subject to the same illness.
Consequently, the reader will expect to encounter a sequence of the
De Remediis Amoris type, where the lover is eventually cured of his
passion, as Boscán indeed is. The reader will expect also the poems
to be exemplificative; in other words, the verses will have to speak
of love in general, a love that is similar to what all men would feel.
According to the artistic precepts of the time, if the poems were
personal and ideosyncratic, the reader would not be able to identify
his state or the situation of other lovers with Boscán's plight. This
exemplificative impetus is one of the major causes of the imper-
sonalness of Boscán's sonnet and *copla* sequences. The poetry in
which contemporary poetic dictates do not require a moral doctrine
— the "Epistle to Diego de Mendoza" for example — presents a
style that is very detailed and personal.

Sonnet V is the first poem in the body of the sequence, so the
poet rightly begins in the first four lines with his birth and first contact with Cupid:

Sonnet V

Aún bien no fui salido de la cuna,

> ni del ama la leche hube dexado,
> quando el amor me tuvo condenado
> a ser de los que siguen su fortuna.   (p.177)

> (I had hardly left the crib,
> nor had I been weaned from the breast,
> when Love had condemned me
> to be one of those that follow his banner.)

Since then he has been subject to Love's whims, and now wonders how such a terrible ill can endure so long; or, if it lasts so long, how it can be so fierce: "Dime: tan fuerte mal ¿cómo es tan largo? / y mal tan largo, di: ¿cómo es tan fuerte?"

In Sonnet VI Boscán defines the kind of love he is going to be experiencing. It is a courtly love, one that takes place in a closed system where there is neither ascent nor descent, but only service.

Sonnet VI

> El alto cielo que en sus movimientos,
> por diversas figuras discurriendo,
> en nuestro sentir flaco está influyendo
> diversos y contrarios sentimientos;
>
>   y una vez mueve blandos pensamientos,
> otra vez asperezas va encendiendo;
> y es su uso traernos revolviendo,
> agora con pesar, y ora contentos.
>
>   Fixo está en mí sin nunca hacer mudanza
> de planeta ni sino en mi sentido,
> clavado en mis tormentos todavía.
>
>   De ver otro hemisferio no he esperanza;
> y así donde una vez me ha anochecido,
> allí me estoy sin esperar el día.   (p. 178)

> (The high heaven, that with its movements
> through diverse signs passes,
> is influencing upon our weak sensibility
> diverse and contrary feelings;
>
>   and sometimes it brings sweet thoughts,
> other times it inflames harsh ones;
> and it is its custom to set us pondering,
> now with sorrow, now with contentment.
>
>   It is fixt in me without ever making a change

> of a planet nor a sign in my senses,
> nailed still in my torments.
>   I have no hope of ever seeing the other hemisphere,
> and thus where once night has fallen for me,
> I am without hope of seeing the day.)

The poem has a typical structure that is quite sophisticated, considering that Boscán was only recently initiated to its use. The first two quartets present a discursive sentence in four pairs of verses that describe the normal effects of Fortune ("el alto cielo") on mankind. He uses well the opposition of good and bad conditions, introducing its first indirectly by referring to the passions as "diversos y contrarios." Boscán then structures the whole of the second quatrain on the polarity, contrasting "blandos" and "asperezas," "pesar" and "contentos." The quatrain is unified in thought, moreover, by the "y" that begins line 7. The first tercet brilliantly contradicts the normal ways of fortune by stating that his luck does not change. Line 9 is given a powerful assertive sense by beginning emphatically with the stress on the first syllable and by having "nunca" in the middle to receive the central sixth-syllable stress. The subject matter of this line continues into the next with a strong enjambment to the objects of the verb: the planets, signatures, and his feelings. The forceful movement is emphasized by the three uses of synalepha in the tercet's first line ("fixo-está-en mi sin nunca-hacer mudanza") and the compact alliterative "sino-en mi sentido" of the next verse. Line 11 serves as a result of the unusual state of his fortune by reporting that his circumstance is "clavado" in his torments. The use of "clavar" refers to the attempt of those who have good fortune to set the brake on the dame's wheel — "echar el clavo a la rueda de la fortuna" — so it will not move downward for them. Boscán ingeniously takes this idea and uses it in precisely the opposite way; the brake has been set on the wheel of fortune for him, but it was set when the wheel was at its nadir. Because of this, he concludes in the last tercet, there is no hope of ever seeing the day again, in other words, of escaping from the moon's influence; for the "luna" is the habitat of "fortuna," as he stated in Sonnet V.

For the poet, then, love is a service that is constant suffering and torment without any hope of relief. The lover obviously does not want it any other way; because if the pain disappeared it would mean that the blazing fires of love which cause the affliction would have died. The poem is therefore totally antiplatonic, for the idea that love is good and that the purpose of love is to ascend to greater and higher levels of spiritual fulfillment is wholly absent; in fact, precisely the opposite is postulated.

This sublimation of the senses to the pangs of love is the predominant note for Sonnets I–LXXVII. Sonnet LI, for example, which is towards the end of this "historia interior" of Boscán's courtly affairs, expresses the same petrified spirit:

Sonnet LI

Quien dice que el ausencia causa olvido,
merece ser de todos olvidado;
el verdadero y firme enamorado
está, quando está ausente, más perdido.

Aviva la memoria su sentido;
la soledad levanta su cuidado;
hallarse de su bien tan apartado,
hace su desear más encendido.

No sanan las heridas en él dadas,
aunque cese el mirar que las causó,
si quedan en el alma confirmadas.

Que si uno está con muchas cuchilladas,
porque huye de quien le acuchilló,
no por eso serán mejor curadas.   (p. 200)

(He who says that absence causes forgetfulness
merits to be forgotten by all;
the true and firm lover
is, when absent, the most lost.

Memory rekindles his spirit;
Loneliness raises his cares;
to find himself so apart from his beloved,
makes his desire more ardent.

The wounds received by him are not cured,
even though the glances that caused them may cease,
if they remain confirmed in the soul.

For if one has many wounds,
just because he flees from one who wounded him,
does not mean they will be better cured.)

The wounds and pain remain even when the lovers are parted,

because Memory and Loneliness (here allegorized as projections
that assault his soul from without) increase the care and sentiment.
The conceptualness of the last tercet, where Boscán literalizes the
wounds of love as stab wounds by a knife that are not cured any
better because he flees his assailant, shows a greater sophistication
and a broader sense of how the sonnet format can be utilized.

Sonnets VII–XXV do not present any notable innovations in
Boscán's technique nor in his experiences with love. Sonnet VII is
an imitation of Petrarch's "Solo e pensoso i più deserti campi";[3]
and in Sonnet VIII the poet finally addresses his "señora." This
one and IX explain how he first began to serve his beloved only to
be almost immediately rejected by her. The rest of the sonnets in
this group describe an unreciprocated love in which the poet strives
to be recognized, then leaves for another city only to be haunted by
the memory of this lady. In Sonnets X–XI, he complains to her, but
to little advantage; so he decides to abandon her service (XII). His
imagination will not allow him to forget her beauty (XIII, a rendition of Petrarch's Sonnet CCLXXIV: "Datemi pace, o duri miei
pensieri"), and he sees that trying to forget her was a mistake
because each step away from her increases his pain (XIV). He
desires to go wherever it would be possible to see his lady (XV, an
imitation of Petrarch's Sonnet CXLV: "Pommi ove 'l sole occide i
piori e l'erba"), for he finds it impossible to live without her (XVI).
He has by now received a bad reputation among his friends due to
his strange conduct, and he has lost contact with the normal
rhythm of life; but no matter how much he now would like to
return to his mistress, fate and habit do not allow him (XVII).

Suddenly, in Sonnet XVIII (inspired by Estramps I of Ausias
March), Boscán discovers a renewed delight in love and announces
it to everyone. It is after this particular sonnet that Boscán inserts
Canciones I and II, which are the only two optimistic *canciones*.
Now he fosters his suffering and affliction (XIX), and when he
thinks upon his love he cries copiously but with joy (XX). Another
cloud covers his happiness in Sonnet XXI, and the third and fourth
canciones that follow the sonnet also express the renewed sad experiences of his affair. Boscán now wonders under what star he was
born to have to suffer so much, and why he has ever had any hope
of success (XXII). He finds no pleasure in love now (XXIII), and
sees that the long absence is wasting his life away (XXIV); so he

decides to break completely the relationship and considers returning his soul to health.

After a moment of vacillation (XXVI–XXVII), the poet again becomes amorously involved with a lady. The close rhythm of the first twenty-five sonnets is not so marked in this second group, but an outline can be perceived. Boscán senses the renewed pangs of love, but doubts their veracity (XXVIII–XXIX). Nevertheless, he timidly pushes forward in the affair, although he repeats in sonnet after sonnet the fear that this love will be as hapless as the first one was (XXX–XLIII). At Sonnet XLIV, Boscán becomes more optimistic and sees that the desire to write in praise of his lady ("la gana de escribir") reinforces the goodness of his love; and, effectively, the next three sonnets (XLV–XLVII) praise the age in which his lady was born. But in Sonnet XLVIII the poet again finds himself apart from his beloved and laments his fate. He tries to feign happiness, but the fires of love reveal his true state (L). He is absent from her (LI) and he wishes desperately that he could flee from his own self (LII). Boscán then describes this state of torment in various ways, seeking to analyze every aspect of his love melancholy, even to the point of turning on his lady to accuse her of being the cause of his troubles (LVII–LIX). The poet finds consolation only in his dreams, as the famous sonnet LXI, which has appeared in so many anthologies,[4] confesses:

Sonnet LXI

Dulce soñar y dulce congoxarme,
quando estaba soñando que soñaba;
dulce gozar con lo que me engañaba,
si un poco más durara el engañarme.

Dulce no estar en mí, que figurarme
podía quanto bien yo deseaba;
dulce placer, aunque me importunaba,
que alguna vez llegaba a despertarme.

¡O sueño! ¡Quánto más leve y sabroso
me fueras, si vinieras tan pesado,
que asentaras en mí con más reposo!

Durmiendo, en fin, fui bienaventurado;
y es justo en la mentira ser dichoso
quien siempre en la verdad fue desdichado. (p. 205)

(Sweet dreams and sweet complaints,

when I was dreaming that I dreamed;
sweet pleasure with which I deceived myself,
that the deceit would last a little longer.
   Sweet to not be in me, to assume that
I could have all the good fortune that I desired;
sweet pleasure, although it bothered me so
that a couple of times it almost woke me.
   Oh dream! how much lighter and tastier
you could be to me if you would come more heavily,
so you could accommodate me with more repose!
   Sleeping, in short, I was fortunate;
and it is just to be happy in the lie
he who was always unhappy in the truth.)

The poem, which is inspired by sonnet LXXXV ("Sogno che dolce-
mente m'hai furato") in Cardinal Bembo's *Rime* (Venice, 1530),
expresses magnificently the soft languidness that one has when he
awakens after a heavenly dream, even to the point of realizing that
the vividness of the images almost awoke the sleeper. The sonnet
displays an ingenious playfulness that is rare in Boscán. The last
tercet closes the piece brilliantly by juxtaposing the frightful reality
of unrequited love with the sweet embraces of the dream. The final
line displays the total awareness by the poet of his true, clearly seen
situation; and yet he has his dream as a reminder of what love could
be like. As Bruce Wardropper commented on the sonnet: "Sleeping
and dreaming create a false state of mind, a deception, a *mentira,*
since they substitute for unpleasant reality an all-pervasive sweetness. The poet, accustomed to the daily anguish of life and love,
feels that he deserves some respite, some happiness, if only in the
unreality of a dream" (*Spanish Poetry,* p. 229). In Sonnet
LXXXII, after his conversion to chaste love, Boscán will use the
same imagery to describe his waking pleasure.
   Sonnets LXII–LXXIV, including the intercalated *Canciones* VII,
VIII, and IX, continue to portray the sad state of Boscán's amorous soul; but in LXXV and LXXVI the poet records a metamorphosis that takes place within him. In the former piece he speaks of
the sweetness of resting at the end of a tempestuous day, and the
pleasure that dawn's splendor gives after the dark night, although
he has to arise and tire himself again. Sonnet LXXVI is more explicit. He foresaw that love wanted to return him again to its prison
as a punishment for his liberated feelings; but he espied the strata-

gem so well that he was able to save himself, because he no longer desires such a certain death.

In Sonnet LXXVII, and in all the others up to Sonnet XC, Boscán declares a new philosophy of love:

Sonnet LXXVII

Otro tiempo lloré, y agora canto;
canto de amor mis bienes sosegados;
de amor lloré mis males tan penados,
que por necesidad era mi llanto.

Agora empieza amor un nuevo canto,
llevando así sus puntos concertados,
que todos, de estar ya muy acordados,
van a dar en un son sabroso y santo.

Razón juntó lo honesto y deleytable,
y de estos dos nació lo provechoso,
mostrando bien de do engendrado fue.

¡O concierto de amor grande y gozoso!
sino que de contento no terné
qué cante, ni qué escriba, ni qué hable.   (p. 213)

(Another time I cried, and now I sing;
I sing about my restful happiness with love,
I wept about my ills with love
that was by necessity my planctus.

Now love begins a new song,
carrying thus its doctrines in concert,
so that all, being now very adjusted,
meet in one soft and saintly sound.

Reason joined the honest and delightful,
and from these two was born the profitable,
showing well from where it was engendered.

Oh concert of great and pleasurable love!
without which I will not have from contentment
what to sing, nor what to write, nor what to speak.)

The emphasis in this sonnet on music, harmony, soft and saintly sound, and concert brings to mind the renewed interest in the Pythagorean "music of the spheres" by the Platonically oriented thinkers of the time.[5] It is a theme that will be picked up by Fray Luis de León in "Oda a Francisco Salinas" and by other Renaissance poets. Boscán avoids any mystical connotations, however, to

concentrate on the musical harmony and balance that his love now
exhibits, as opposed to the earlier laws of "diversos y contrarios
sentimientos" described in Sonnet VI.

Another theme that Boscán introduces in this poem was also
highly esteemed by the contemporary Platonists. The idea that love
is useful, delightful, and honest in varying degrees is stated in León
Hebreo's famous *Dialogues of Love,* and it is repeated numerous
times in the pastoral novels of the later Renaissance.[6] Boscán takes
the three categories and creates of their triple union an image of
perfect love. His desire is not only honest and delightful because
reason has taken control of his faculties, but useful as well; for it
permits him to sing, to write, and to speak.

The notion that a new love has given a new song for the poet to
sing is continued in the next piece:

Sonnet LXXVIII

Antes terné que cante blandamente,
pues amo blandamente, y soy amado;
sé que en amor no es término forzado,
sólo escribir aquel que dolor siente.
    Desaváhase quien está doliente,
y canta en la prisión el desdichado,
con hierros y cadenas fatigado;
mas su cantar del nuestro es diferente.
    Yo cantaré conforme al avecilla,
que canta así a la sombra de algún ramo,
que el caminante olvida su camino,
    quedando trasportado por oílla.
Así yo de ver quien me ama y a quien amo,
en mi cantar terné gozo contino.   (p. 214)

(I have it best to sing delicately,
since I love delicately, and I am loved;
I know that in love it is not a necessary end
to write about only things which express pain.
    He who is in pain airs his woes,
and the unfortunate one sings in prison
fatigued with irons and chains,
but our song is different.
    I will sing like the little bird,
that sings so well in the shadow of some branch,
that the wanderer forgets his way,

> being transported from hearing it.
> Thus I from seeing who loves me and whom I love,
> in my singing I will have continual pleasure.)

This is the first time that Juan Boscán has declared "soy amado." He now knows that all love songs are not about pain and sorrow, for they can also express the delicate pleasure of love; and his ardor is no longer tied to the appetites, which disturb the body and bind the will of the lover. This desire liberates the poet to sing, not like the prisoner in jail, but like the free birds in the trees. Totally absent from this new poetry are the antitheses, the paradoxes, the "negative way," the closed circle of thought, and many of the other poetic structural devices that Boscán used to express his Aristotelian love. It is a total renewal of both language and structure to express a totally new kind of affection.

For one thing, there is the initiation of the simile, in which the poet likens his state to one in nature (this is the first sonnet in which Boscán compares his actions to those in the natural world). There is likewise a specific utilization of syllabic stress, interspersing emphatic, sapphic, and melodic lines with the normal heroic ones to form the following pattern: sheemhhsssshhs. Lines 3 and 4 also participate somewhat in the sapphic stress, since there is accent on the fourth syllable. Boscán also breaks the sacrosanct 4-4-3-3 pattern of the sonnet to use a 4-4-4-2 structure by terminating the penultimate statement at line 12 rather than at line 11. This structure allows the poet to present a terser thought in the final pair of lines. Lope de Vega will later employ the 4-4-4-2 structure repeatedly; but no Spanish poets will alter the traditional rhyme scheme of the Petrarchan sonnet as did the English poeteers when, under the tutorage of Shakespeare, they adopted the scheme of three quatrains and a rhymed couplet.

In the following sonnets the poet exults in his new contentment and secure position (LXXIX), which seems like a miracle to him (LXXX); for the love that once persecuted his soul now heaps a thousand graces on him. He now wants to remain in his present state, as against the earlier love from whose lowly estate he continually attempted to escape; and, more surprisingly for Boscán, he feels absolutely no fear that his good fortune will pass (LXXXI).

The complete peace he now feels is admirably expressed in Sonnet LXXXII, where he employs the adjective "dulce" to begin seven of the lines in a crescendo of perfect love that moves from "sweet repose," "sweet pleasure," "sweet wisdom," to "sweet gratification," "sweet remembering in my breast," "sweet pleasures," "sweet thoughts that I am in Paradise."

Sonnet LXXXII

Dulce reposo de mi entendimiento;
dulce placer fundado sobre bueno;
dulce saber, que de saber soy lleno,
pues tengo de mi bien conocimiento.

Dulce gozar de un dulce sentimiento,
viendo mi cielo estar claro y sereno,
y dulce revolver sobre mi seno,
con firme concluir, que estoy contento.

Dulce gustar de un no sé qué sin nombre,
que amor dentro en mi alma poner quiso,
quando mi mal sanó con gran renombre.

Dulce pensar que estoy en paraíso,
sino que en fin me acuerdo que soy hombre,
y en las cosas del mundo tomo aviso.   (p. 216)

(Sweet repose of my understanding;
sweet pleasure founded on the good;
sweet wisdom, for I am full of wisdom,
since I have recognition of my well-being.

Sweet gratification of a sweet sentiment,
seeing my heaven to be clear and serene;
and sweet remembering in my breast
with firm conclusion that I am content.

Sweet pleasure of an I don't know what without a name,
that love wished to put within my soul,
when it cured my illness with great renown.

Sweet thoughts that I am in Paradise,
and that finally I remember that I am human
and that I take warning from all worldly things.)

He thus uses here a lexicon not seen in his earlier poetry, such as "reposo," "placer," "gozar," "claro," "sereno," "contento," "gustar," "Paraíso." All describe a state of joyful peace he had not experienced before; and which he would not have been able to express with the old courtly lexicon even if he had experienced it. The only other poem that partook in any way of this language was

Sonnet LXI, when the poet dreamed that he was with his lady but awoke at the end to the harsh reality of his misfortune.

Of more importance for the Platonic context, this poem eschews the idea of love as an act of the will and as a physical malady brought on by passion to embrace the notion that love is knowledge, an act of the rational faculties; hence the importance of the words "entendimiento" and "saber" and "conocimiento." The sonnet expresses a sophisticated mental state of psychic consolidation of the poet's being that even Garcilaso de la Vega will not achieve, yet that jibes closely, albeit on a secular plane, with the state of repose described in the mystical songs of San Juan de la Cruz and Fray Luis de León.

Sonnet LXXXIII reflects on how badly he suffered in the early years at the hands of love, and how he has at last won the final battle to become the victor in the long war: "Mi guerra convirtió en tanta victoria / que agora vencedor estoy triunfando, / dexando escrita en todos larga historia" (p. 216). Sonnets LXXXIV-LXXXIX form three pairs of poems which apotheosise his love. In LXXXIV-V Boscán expresses the Neoplatonic theory that love is naturally good, and that it is a fire that burns inside us;[7] but it is a pure and simple fire positioned in its proper sphere. This proper heat warms and illuminates the soul, causing the universe to appear in continual Spring. Sonnets LXXXVI-VII again reflect on how sorely Boscán suffered from the wrong kind of love; now, however, even the thought of the past sadnesses gladdens him. In Sonnets LXXXVIII-IX Boscán arrives at the height of his earthly love, spiritually inhabiting Mount Olympus, where there are no clouds, no storms, no night; for he now possesses a "claro amor" as opposed to the "crudo amor" of his earlier years: "Un claro amor que el alma me ha ilustrado, / con la clara virtud que en mí concibe" (Sonnet LXXXIX, p. 215). He is finally free from the torments of courtly love, and hangs his prison irons in the temple as a memorial to his rebirth.

The last sonnet in the sequence summarizes his attainment of "casto amor" and his recovery from the sickness of courtly love:

Sonnet XC

De una mortal y triste perlesía,
en su cama tendida mi alma estaba;
y como el mal los nervios le ocupaba,

ni de pies ni de manos se valía.
El casto amor, que Dios del cielo envía,
le dixo en ver la pena que pasaba;
'Suelta tus pies, tus manos te destraba,
toma tu lecho acuestas, y haz tu vía.'
Volví luego a mirarme, y vime sano,
y caminé sin rastro de dolencia,
por las cuestas así como en lo llano.
¡O poder eternal y soberano!
¿Quién sanará con propia diligencia,
si la salud no da tu larga mano?   (p. 220)

(With a mortal and sad disease,
my soul was stretched out in bed;
and since the sickness occupied its nerves,
it could not move its feet nor its hands.
Chaste love, that God sent from heaven,
told it, on seeing the pain it was suffering:
"Free your feet, unfetter your hands,
take your bed on your back, and go your way."
I looked then at myself again, and I saw myself healthy,
and I walked without a trace of pain,
over the hills as well as along the plain.
¡Oh eternal and sovereign power!
Who will be cured with proper diligence
if Your generous hand does not give health?)

It is a simple four-part sonnet. The first quatrain relates the state of his paralyzed soul, and the spiritual nature of the sickness is emphasized poetically by a strong hyperbaton in the first two lines which reverses the normal word order: "Mi alma estaba tendida en la cama de una mortal y triste perlesía." The poem thus allegorizes the soul and gives a spiritual sense to the action. The mention of the paralysis of the hands and feet lends a human and realistic quality to the allegory. The second quatrain presents the remedy to the sickness outlined in the first. Line 5 states bluntly that Chaste Love (also allegorized) spoke to his invalid soul and told it to rise up and walk. The reference to feet and hands in line 7 and to the bed in line 8 unites this quatrain linguistically to the first one, where the same terms are used. The source is the numerous New Testament references to Jesus' remark "take up your bed and walk" in Matthew 9:6, Mark 2:9, Luke 5:24, and John 5:8. The biblical allusion adds to spiritualize further the event. The first tercet describes the poet's miraculous cure of the paralysis and pain; and the last tercet is an encomium to the eternal Power for returning him to health.

The tone and the religious spirit of the sonnet classify it as another "Conversión de Boscán," functioning in relation to the sonnets in the same way as the "Conversión" functioned in relation to the *coplas*. The major difference is of course the quality of the religious emotion. In the "Conversión" Boscán returned to the Catholic faith and repented of all earthly desires and needs. He explained this conversion as a movement from death of the soul because of the dominance of passion to death of the body through communion of the sacraments and the remembrance of God (*Memoria Dei*), death (*Memento mori*), and his own creatureliness. In this sonnet, the conversion is totally different, although the tone is similar. Here the poet is converted from one kind of love ("crudo amor," "el mal") to another kind ("casto amor," "el bien"). He has learned, as he said in Sonnet LXXXIV, that "amor es bueno en sí naturalmente"; but it must be love of the proper fire, a fire "puro y simple y puesto allá en su esfera" (Sonnet LXXXV), rather than a fire that consumes the spiritual substance of the courtier. In short, the love must be of a pastoral-Platonic nature, as is going to be described two decades later in the novels of Jorge de Montemayor, Gaspar Gil Polo, Lope de Vega, and Cervantes. The differences between these two kinds of love cannot be overemphasized, because they are what separate more than anything else the medieval spirit from the Renaissance spirit. The total divergence of the two types of love is perhaps best seen in the development of the amorous novel in Spain. Enrique Moreno Baez describes the transition in the following manner:

I believe that the difference between one love and the other is in the fact that for the Platonist love is a virtue of the understanding and the only path to achieve knowledge of the Ideas and therefore even the Supreme Good, while the sentimental novel, late fruit of Gothic culture, is based on the Scholastic concept of love, a passion of the concupiscible appetite that, although it can be resisted by free will or moderated by volition, frequently dominates the will, obfuscating the understanding, even to the point that the bad is taken for the good. Such a disorder of our potencies is what gives to these sentimental novels that tormentuous and stormy air that contrasts so much with the serene melancholy of the pastoral novels, where even the tears are melodious and are subjected to a rhythm and cadence, as is the verse and music. In other words, if for the latter love is a cognitive virtue, for the former it is a sickness of the soul, that in many cases leads to death.[8]

It is without question that the recognition of Boscán's greatness could rest solely on his miraculous ability to make the radical shift from the Aristotelian world of love as a physical orexis to the Platonic universe of love as a spiritual condition. Of all the poets and novelists in the Christian world, Juan Boscán was the one who most successfully inhabited both the medieval and the Renaissance realms of existence and who demonstrated in his poetry the absolute divergence of the one from the other.

II   *Italianate Canciones*

Juan Boscán was the first Spaniard to utilize the *canzone.* The form, sometimes termed "estancia" in Spanish, is quite flexible, and Boscán experimented with almost every type. His eleven extant *canciones,* one of which is thought to be spurious, all differ either in meter or in verse distribution. The *canción* is made up of unlimited numbers of stanzas of from thirteen to eighteen lines each with seven or eleven syllables; and there are no set rules as to which lines have to be short or long. The rhyme scheme most favored by Boscán, for he used it in *Canciones* I, IX, and X, is the fifteen-line stanza rhyming abcbaccdeedfdff. Even here, though, the distribution of seven and eleven syllable lines is different. In I the rhyme is aBCbACCDEeDfDFF, and in the other two the scheme is ABCBACCDEeDfDFF.

An additional characteristic of the *canción* is that each stanza has a *capo,* a *corpo,* and a *coda.*[9] The *capo* is the first group of six or seven lines (the first seven lines in *Canción* I, for example); the *corpo* is the central group (consisting of six lines in I); and the *coda* is the last two or three verses. The distribution of the *capo* and the *corpo* does not have to be the same within a *canción.* In X, for instance, some stanzas are 7-6-2 while others are 6-7-2. The poet employs these groups of verses to form his sequence of ideas in much the same way as the 4-4-3-3 format of the sonnet is used.

Another method used by some critics — Enrique Segura Covarsi[10] and Thaddeus C. Porter[11] with Boscán's poetry in particular — to describe the stanzaic structure of the *canción* is with the terms *piedi, chiave, sirima,* and *comiato.* The *piedi* are the first groups of three or four lines in the poem. *Canciones* I–IV and VIII–X, according to this system, all have two *piedi* of three lines; while V–VII each has two *piedi* of four lines. The *chiave* is a one line "key" in the middle of the strophe. Boscán does not often emphasize the middle lines in his poetry. The final lines are subsumed under the term *sirima;* and the *comiato* is the group of verses at the end of the entire *canción* where the poet directs himself to the poem. The *comiato* — or "remate," as it is called in Spanish — for *Canción* I reads: "Canción, si de muy larga te culparen, / respóndeles que sufran con paciencia / que un gran dolor a todo da licencia" ("Song, if they blame you for being too long, / respond that they should suffer with patience / for a great pain gives licence for all"). Although these two systems are similar, the terms *capo, corpo,* and *coda* fit better Boscán's stanzas and will be the ones employed here.

The syllabic accent of the hendecasyllables in a *canción* is normally the same as in a sonnet, falling on the second, sixth, and tenth syllables. The accent usually is on the second and sixth syllable of the short lines. The *canción* thus offers the poet a very flexible verse form and allows him a freedom of expression not found in any of the Castilian meters. It will be the favorite form for longer non-epic poems until the introduction of the *silva,* which differs from its predecessor only in that there is no limit to the lines in a stanza.

According to J. P. Wickersham Crawford, Boscán's *canciones* reflect the same autobiography of love as do the *coplas* and the sonnets. The first two deal with the earlier love affair, and the last eight *canciones* treat the poet's state of mind as mirrored in Sonnets XXVIII–LXXVI, and include frequent verbal similarities with them ("Chronology," p. 34). Thaddeus C. Porter sees an even closer sequence of events in the ten *canciones:*

Briefly stated, Boscán's first song tells of the beginning of his love and the suffering associated with that love. In the second, the poet is absent from his lady. He laments this absence and tells some of his fantasies concerning her. The third song contains vague references to her beauty and restates his agitation and uncertainty with regard to her. The fourth continues to describe the poet's changed condition. He wants to live and die, to speak and remain silent, to be with his beloved and to be absent from her. The

fifth song tells of the poet's futile efforts to find happiness in memories of
the past or contemplation of the present. In the sixth, his suffering continues. Death, sudden death, would be a relief. In the seventh, his agitation continues. He cannot decide what course to pursue. The eighth song
finds the poet vacillating between hope and despair, courage and coward-
ice. His plea becomes stronger for her to return his love. The ninth is a pre-
palinode as the poet reviews his life, still suffering from the deceitful
nature of love. The tenth and last song is Boscán's palinode. He recognizes
and acknowledges the errors of his past life, turns to God for forgiveness
and becomes another Lazarus. (p. 129)

While it is true that all ten *canciones* belong to the earlier pre-
Platonic period (the first nine poems are intercalated among
Sonnets XVIII–LXVII, and the last one comes at the end of Book
Two), there is no basis for the assumption that the first two were
written earlier than the others, nor that the songs present a cumula-
tive account of Boscán's love. *Canción* I is clearly the introductory
poem, and *Canción* X is logically the last; but II–IX all express the
same attitude towards love. The songs, in sum, are *rime sparse* that
form part of the sonnet sequence in precisely the same way that
Petrarch's *canzoni* made up part of his sequence.

Canción I, which comprises thirty-one stanzas of fifteen lines
each, has one of the most assertive initial strophes in Boscán's
poetic corpus:

Canción I

1.   Quiero hablar un poco;
     mas teme el corazón de fatigarse,
     porque si hablo, sé que será tanto,
     que el seso ha de alterarse,
     y a su culpa no es bien tornarse loco.
     Tras esto mostrarse ha mi crudo llanto
     tal, que con él no querría dar espanto.
     Pero pasar este peligro es fuerza,
     y escójolo por menos peligroso;
     de suerte que si oso,
     es ya por el aprieto que me fuerza;
     y el alma ha de probar
     su seso y su poder, y así se esfuerza.
     Con esto tales cosas he de hablar,
     que aun ora estoy pensando de callar.   (p.222)

(I want to speak a while;
but the heart fears of tiring itself,
because if I speak, I know it will be so much
that I will go out of my mind,
and for its sake it is not a good idea to go mad.
Following this my harsh weeping must show itself
so, that I would not want to frighten with it.
But it is necessary to undertake this danger,
and I choose it for being less dangerous;
for if I dare,
it is now for the situation that forces me;
and the soul has to prove
its wisdom and its power, and thus it makes the effort.
I therefore have to speak such things,
that even now I am thinking about being silent.)

This forceful introduction, beginning with the "Quiéro-hablár un póco," then drawing back with the "mas téme-el corazón," sets the course for the entire collection of *canciones*. As in Sonnets I–IV, the poet is imprisoned by love and cannot escape, yet he feels an obligation to write about his sad affair, although the effort may derange his mind. Moreover, it is less dangerous than remaining silent, which would surely totally destroy him. The sense of fear and hesitation on the part of the poet is admirably expressed in the short phrases (seven of them end in a semicolon or period) and the use of "mas," "tras esto," "pero," and "con esto." The first stanza thus establishes the courtly tone of suffering, fear, danger of losing one's life, but necessity to verbalize one's pain that runs throughout the collection.

The second stanza continues the thought pattern of the initial verses by repeating the linguistic structure of the preceding stanza's first two lines, but stating the opposite.

2.   Callaré si pudiere;
mas no podré, que ha mucho que no puedo.
Hablaré por no estarme como estoy,
pues no puedo estar quedo,
que mal sosegará quien así muere.
Si parto, sólo por irme me voy,
mudanzas hago, por no ser quien soy;
en fin, pues esto tanto ya conviene,
comenzaré a quexarme a pesar mío.

Mas quizá es desvarío
llanto que en tal dolor tan tarde viene.
Eslo, mas mi tristura
¿qué hará si otro remedio no tiene?
Hallo asimismo en tanta desventura,
que el seso y la razón es ya locura.   (p. 223)

> (I will be silent if I can;
> but I won't be able to, for it has been a long time since I can't.
> I will speak so I won't be as I am,
> since I can't remain quiet,
> for one who dies that way is badly consoled.
> If I leave, I will go away solely to go away;
> I will make changes in order not to be who I am;
> in short, since this now suits my purpose,
> I will begin to complain to my own regret.
> But perhaps it is a derangement,
> crying that comes so late for such pain.
> It is, but my sadness,
> what will it do if it has no other remedy?
> I find myself nevertheless with so much bad fortune,
> that the mind and reason are now mad.)

This stanza also follows the first one in its hesitating style, here seen in no less than eight sentence divisions. Almost every line is a thought in itself, giving the verses a halting rhythm that objectifies the poet's fearfully nervous state of mind. The poet is trapped, moreover, by his lack of decisiveness. He cannot be silent and he cannot talk, nor can he remain nor can he stay; and the indecision quite simply drives him mad. Adjectives are totally lacking in both stanzas, with the sole exception of "crudo" to describe his weeping.

The third stanza continues the poet's interior struggle as to whether or not he should write of his affairs, and the fourth again expresses the pain it is going to give him:

> 4. Olvidando el comienzo, el fin no hallo.
>   Mal concierto terná cuento tan largo,
>   do todo ha sido amargo:
>   y agora lo ha de ser también contallo.   (p. 224)

> (Forgetting the beginning, I do not find the end.

Such a long story will have a bad ending,
for all has been bitter:
and now the telling it is going to be bitter also.)

This fourth stanza closes the introductory part of the *canción* by stating the necessary moral: "Mi alma sólo queda / por escarmiento a muchos amadores" ("My soul alone remains / as a warning to many lovers").

The remainder of *Canción* I is the "tan gran historia" (stanza 4) of Boscán's courtly loves. He explains how he first felt the sting of love and wondered if he alone was experiencing such feelings. He found himself doing and saying things that had never before occurred to him, especially fear of not seeing his lady, and he thought that perhaps he should cure his wounds; but it was already too late. From then forward the affair brought only torments. First came jealousy, then his imagination turned on him. He finally forced himself to declare his love to the damsel, and she rejected him. The poet pours out the feelings he had after this terrible blow, and sees death as his only consolation. He finally realizes that the more he writes, the more he suffers; so he closes with the decision to be silent for a while.

Canciones IV–IX are all expressions in much the same way of this unrequited love. Their tone and language are the same as in *Canción* I, Sonnets I–LXXVI, and the Castilian verses. The only two *canciones* that differ are II and III. The latter, which was inspired by Petrarch's *Canzone* seventy-two ("Gentil mia donna, i' veggio"), is innovative in that it is epistolary. Boscán addresses his "Gentil Señora mía" (first line) and declares his love and service to her. He praises her beauty and explains what good fortune it would be for him if she should respond favorably, although he fears that she may reject his courtship. The *remate* expresses his hope for a reply to his letter. Because *Canción* III describes Boscán's amorous expectations rather than his unrequited love, it has a gentler and more refined tone than the other poems. The poem is also noteworthy for its brevity, since it has only seven stanzas of fifteen lines each.

Canción II is also different from the other poems. It expresses the thoughts of a shepherd absent from his beloved. He remembers their parting moments, but wonders what she is doing now, if she is thinking of him or perhaps laughing about his love for her. The

poem ends rather optimistically, with the shepherd's expectation of
seeing her again soon. The verse form is the only one in which there
are more short lines than hendecasyllables: abCabCcdeeDfF. The
subject matter comes from Petrarch's *Canzone* one hundred
twenty-six. The most outstanding aspect of this song is the new and
refreshing description of nature by Boscán, based principally on
the multiple use of adjectives and the flowing quality of the seven-
syllable line. The first stanza is the best example:

Canción II

1.   Claros y frescos ríos
      que mansamente vais
      siguiendo vuestro natural camino;
      desiertos montes míos,
      que en un estado estáis
      de soledad muy triste de contino;
      aves, en quien hay tino
      de descansar cantando;
      árboles que vivís,
      y en fin también morís,
      y estáis perdiendo a tiempos y ganando;
      ¡oídme juntamente
      mi voz amarga, ronca y tan doliente!   (p. 238)

      (Clear and fresh rivers
      that calmly go
      following your natural course;
      my desert hills
      that are in a state
      of continuous very sad solitude;
      birds, in whom there is skill
      to rest by singing;
      trees that live,
      and finally also die,
      and are losing and gaining with the seasons;
      listen to me together
      my harsh, rough and so painful voice!)

The poet has achieved here his most lyrical expressiveness through
the use of alliteration, enjambment, and antithesis. The first two
lines are formed of symmetrical vowels:

a-o-i-e-o-i-o
e-a-a-e-e-a

To these flowing vowels he adds three *os* sounds and the *r* sound in the first line and a strong *m* sound twice in line two to create an onomatopoeic equivalent of the bubbling but quietly running stream. The third hendecasyllabic line adds to the idea of movement by employing just four three-syllable words (one has a diphthong) without pause; so all three lines form by enjambment one continuous motion in imitation of the river. The form thus admirably restates the content of the verses. The next three lines describe the uninhabited mountains in the same way. The first of the three verses presents the apostrophe to the mountains with four *s* sounds and a strong repetitive *m,* and the next line begins "que" to run until the end of the group, expressing thereby the continuousness of the sad solitude stated in the last words: "de contino." Boscán further lyricizes the verses by using a repetitive rhyme in the middle line: "Estado estáis." The *capo* of the stanza thus presents two perfectly formed three line *piedi*.

The *corpo* consists of two lines invoking the birds and three lines directed to the trees. Line 8 again employs a repetitive rhyme ("des*cansa*r *canta*ndo") to express the singing of the birds; and the three verses dedicated to the trees use a sophisticated antithesis that unites the lines with a 1-1-2 pattern:

> arboles que *vivís*[a]
> y en fin también *morís*[b]
> y estáis *perdiendo*[b] a tiempos y *ganando*[a]

Here too the enjambment, the pauseless hendecasyllabic line, and the use of the present progressive tense give a sense of movement associated with the passing of time. All four apostrophes in the *capo* and the *corpo,* in effect, present a continuous movement of some form: the bubbling brook, the mountains in perpetual solitude, the birds singing, and the trees losing their leaves and sprouting new ones with the seasons.

The *coda* breaks sharply with these soft and melancholic evocations by beginning with a hard command ("Oídme") and by employing three rough sounding words that express the opposite sensations: "amarga," "ronca," "doliente." There is no alliteration here, nor any intralinear rhyme. The words are hard and bitter

and declare forcefully that the poet's emotional situation is quite
contrary to the pastoral setting he has described. Coming as they do
at the end of the stanza, the sharp words give an element of surprise
to the verses, jolting the reader by way of contrast into a clear
awareness of the poet's suffering.
A comparison of the stanza with Petrarch's first stanza will
show, moreover, that the excellence of the Spanish verses is
Boscán's own work:

> Chiare, fresche, e dolci acque,
> ove le belle membra
> pose colei che sola a me par donna;
> gentil ramo ove piacque
> (con sospir mi rimembra)
> a lei di fare al bel fianco colonna;
> erba e fior, che la gonna
> leggiadera ricoverse
> co l'angelico seno;
> aere sacro, sereno,
> ove Amor co' begli occhi il cor m'asperse;
> date udienzia insieme
> a le dolenti mie parole estreme.

Another innovative and equally lyrical stanza is the following:

> 10.   Tengo en el alma puesto
>   su gesto tan hermoso,
>   y aquel saber estar adonde quiera;
>   el recoger honesto,
>   el alegre reposo,
>   el no sé qué de no sé qué manera;
>   y con llaneza entera
>   el saber descansado,
>   el dulce trato hablando,
>   el acudir callando,
>   y aquel grave mirar disimulado.
>   Todo esto está ausente,
>   y otro tiempo lo tuve muy presente.   (p. 242)

> (I have placed in my soul
> her so beautiful gesture,
> and that knowing how to be where she desires;
> the honest disposition,

> the happy repose,
> the I don't know what of I don't know what demeanor;
> and with complete unaffectedness
> the restful wisdom;
> the sweet way of speaking,
> the succoring by being quiet,
> and that grave disimulated look.
> All this is absent,
> and another time I had it very present.)

This exceptionally fine stanza expresses admirably the new spirit in Boscán's poetry. The lines flow one after the other in a harmonious balance. The first verse gives the subject, verb, and preposition of place ("tengo en el alma puesto") and is the formative structure for the *capo* and *corpo,* in which nine objects are presented. The *coda* summarizes the above with the initial "todo," then gives the sad fact that the objects are absent ("ausente"), only to present the antithetical "presente" in the last line. The last line also is linked to the first one by using "tener" in the first person and by explaining the first line: the poet has this all spiritually in his soul because what he earlier had physically present is now absent. The flowing quality of the stanza is achieved by the repetition of linguistic structures in the short lines ("el" followed by an adjective and a noun) and by using similar structures also in the third and the third from the last lines ("y aquel saber estar adonde quiera / ... / y aquel grave mirar disimulando"). These lines rightly separate the first two and the last two, which is the *coda.* The middle line, called the *chiave,* is the famous verse that has been attributed, although with much controversy, to be the source for the line "un no sé qué que queda balbuciendo" of San Juan de la Cruz.[12]

Canción X, which is the final poem in Book Two, is the palinode to the other pieces, as the "Conversión" was to the *coplas* and Sonnet XC was to that sequence. The *canción* is closer to the palinode of the *coplas* in that it expresses a totally religious conversion rather than a movement of the soul to a more spiritual kind of love. Boscán describes how Love led him by the hand for many years, placating the pain and torment with moments of amorous satisfaction. During that time the poet experienced neither fear nor jealousy because he was so confident of his love; although he later suffered all the sad misfortunes that befall courtly lovers. Yet God, who shed His blood for us, cures all ills and wounds; and while at times He allows many to suffer intolerable pain, it is only to resuscitate them later as He did Lazarus:

Canción X

5.   Tú, Dios, con tu sentencia
me enterraste en dolores tan continos,
porque después me diese tu clemencia
que otro Lázaro fuese en tu presencia.   (p. 279)

(You, God, with Your judgment
You buried me in such continuous pain,
in order to give me Your clemency afterwards
to have another Lazarus in Your presence.)

As in the "Conversión," Boscán describes his new self in terms of the proper functioning of the three potencies of the soul:

7.   Valdráme la memoria si el mal viene
a tentarme por donde me ha tentado.
La voluntad de verse libre y suelta,
guardarse ha de revuelta.
El entender por prueba habrá alcanzado,
que es mengua y dolor grave,
cativamente siempre estar atado.   (p. 280)

(Memory will aid me if the ills return
to tempt me from where they have tempted me.
Will, seeing itself free and unbound,
will guard itself from sedition.
Understanding will have perceived as proof,
that it is debasing and grave pain
to be always tied as a prisoner.)

He closes by declaring that his soul is now at peace with his desire: "Nunca quise sino lo que aora tengo, / que es tener en muy poco lo que es poco, / y poder sosegar mi pensamiento" (pp. 280–81). The poet therefore feels able to show to others the harsh road along which he has come, how he lost his way and walked alone without direction, and how divine grace took away his foolishness and error:

10. Lo que puedo mostrar a todo el mundo
es, que me perdí yo en este camino,
y que anduve por él siempre perdido,
Perdíme al primer paso, y al segundo
estuve ya del todo tan sin tino,
que en lo peor quedé quasi tendido.
Mi alma por allí pasar no vido
a hombre vivo en quien se guareciese;
y si alguno pasó, tiró adelante,
sin parar un instante,
hasta que yo de vista le perdiese.
Así quedé, mas vino
primero que del todo anocheciese,
quien con la gracia del poder divino
el error me quitó y el desatino. (p. 281)

    (What I can show to everyone
is that I lost myself on this highway,
and I walked always lost along it.
I became lost with the first step, and with the second
I was already so completely without direction,
that I remained almost stretched out in the worst place.
My soul did not see pass by there
any man who would give aid;
and if someone passed by, he kept marching forward,
without stopping for an instant,
until I would lose him from sight.
Thus I remained, but He came along
before the night completely closed me in,
Who with the grace of His divine power
took from me my error and folly.)

The indirect analogy of Boscán's plight with that described by Jesus in the parable of the Good Samaritan (Luke 10:30) gives this last strophe a strong religious overtone. Like the man from Jerusalem who was beaten by thieves and left to die, Boscán was wounded by love and abandoned to his fate. None of his friends would stop to help him, until finally the "Good Samaritan" came to his aid, which in all figurative literature is equated to Christ's succor to the Gentiles. The technique is not new in Boscán's poetry, since in this same *canción* he compared himself to Lazarus, and in Sonnet XC he described his soul as a paralytic who was told to take up his bed and walk. The analogy always strikes a sensitive note in the mind of

the Christian reader, however, because all three New Testament
references are about people who suffered cruelly at the hands of
fortune — the "old" law, according to the theologians — but who
were redeemed by the only person capable of curing them because
only He brings the "new" law of grace.

The curing of the paralysis, death, and wounds of course ties in
magnificently with the Aristotelian-Thomistic idea that love is a
sickness, a disease of the soul that wastes the flesh of the lover and
distracts his mind. This infirmity is cured here by divine grace. In
Sonnet XC it was cured by "casto amor," although the Gospel
references were even more direct. In the "Epistle to Mendoza" the
palliation of the malady will again be described, but there the cura-
tive will be married love couched in classical topoi of the retired
life, the golden mean, ataraxia, and virtue.

CHAPTER 4

The Third Book: Later Works

THE third book of Boscán's poetry contains the short epic "Historia de Leandro y Hero," a love poem entitled simply "Capítulo I," a courtly letter entitled "Epístola," the "Epístola de don Diego de Mendoza a Boscán" and the "Respuesta de Boscán a don Diego de Mendoza," and a light piece entitled "Octava rima." These works, with the exception of perhaps "Epístola," were assuredly written after 1533. They are imbued with a Neoplatonism and a classical humanism that is nowhere found in the earlier works. In effect, the inspiration for the three Books of Boscán's poetry can be generalized as being from the *cancionero* tradition for Book One, from the Petrarchan school for Book Two, and from the Italian and Latin humanists for Book Three.

I   *"Leander and Hero"*

"Leandro y Hero" is the most outstanding product of Boscán's humanist training. It is a continuous 2,793-line poem in blank verse, and it is one of the earliest uses of that form in Spanish, preceded only by Garcilaso's "Epístola a Boscán" (1534). The meter requires simply that each line have eleven syllables. There is no end-rhyme, nor are there any standards for the number of lines in a stanza. The rhythm of the poem thus depends on the hendecasyllabic beat, internal rhyme, alliteration, repetition of words, parallelization, bimembrations, and other poetic devices. Blank verse imitates the Horatian dactylic hexameter, but it lacks of course the rhythmic feet of the latter. It was Boscán's blank verse, by the way, that the Baroque poet Luis de Góngora found so dull (see the quotation from "De la Fabúla de Leandro y Hero" in Knapp, p. 474).

According to Arnold G. Reichenberger, there are four different
parts to the poem, and four different strains of sources: "(1)
Musaeus provided the outline of the story and (2) Ovid's two
Heroides (XVIII and XIX), *Hero Leandro* and *Leander Heroni,*
tinged Boscán's psychological analysis of the two lovers. With
these basic sources are combined (3) two episodes from Virgil's
Georgics, IV, 315–567, the legend of Aristaeus and the origin of bee
raising, which itself is tied up in Virgil with the Orpheus and Eurydice story, and finally (4) Proteus' complaint before Neptune about
the rough treatment he received at the hands of Aristaeus, when the
youth wrested from him the secret of how to appease the irate
spirits who killed his bees, a story for which no source has been
identified."[1]

The major source is clearly the short three hundred forty-three
line poem entitled *Hero and Leander* by the Greek writer Musaeus
(fl. A.D. fifth century). The work was unknown in the Middle
Ages, and was first brought to Italy after the fall of Constan-
tinople. The earliest extant manuscript is a copy done in 1464 by
Constantine Lascaris. The *editio princeps* was undertaken by the
Aldine Press in 1494. It became an immediate best-seller, probably
because the publishers included a Latin translation of the Greek
text on the facing pages. The first Spanish edition of the original
Greek was done by Demetrius Ducas at Alcalá de Henares around
1514. It is not impossible that Boscán used this Greek text, since he
apparently knew the idiom. In the "Privilegio" to his poetry, it is
stated that among the papers he left unedited was a tragedy of
Euripedes (p. 7 in Knapp). Since Euripedes was not published in
translation anywhere before 1544, Boscán must have done his
rendition from the original work.

Boscán was only one of the many authors who translated
Musaeus' tale. The Italian poet Bernardo Tasso had published in
1537 a *Favola di Leandro ed Ero* that Boscán used as a source for
his own version. In France, Clement Marot published a translation
in 1541, and towards the end of the century B. Baldi did an Italian
version (1590) and Christopher Marlowe put the poem into English
(1593). None of these versions is near the length of Boscán's, since
the translators deviated little from the original Greek.

The legend of Leander and Hero was of course known to the
western world long before Musaeus' manuscript was brought to
Italy. Virgil alludes to the tragic couple in Book III of the *Georgics*

(vv. 258–63), and Ovid writes extensively on the legend in the two *Heroides* used by Boscán to expand on the Greek text. There are also a couple of epigrams by Martial on the subject, which Boscán also entered into his poem.

The evidence points to Boscán as the first Spaniard to treat seriously the theme of Hero and Leander. Garcilaso de la Vega wrote a precious sonnet about Leander's fatal crossing of the Hellespont ("Pasando el mar Leandro el animoso"), which was published before Boscán's tale, and Gutierre de Cetina, Francisco Sa de Miranda, Juan Coloma, and Jorge de Montemayor, all younger contemporaries of Boscán, composed sonnets on the topic. They were followed by poems from the pens of almost every major poet of the Spanish Golden Age. Marcelino Menéndez Pelayo compiled an extensive bibliography of these works and listed no less than sixty-three different poetic pieces dedicated to the two lovers (*Boscán,* pp. 314–30). Menéndez Pelayo's work was substantiated, amplified, and anthologized by Francisca Moya del Baño in *El tema de Hero y Leandro en la literatura española* (Murcia: Universidad de Murcia, 1966). Moya published all the important Spanish contributions to the theme, except for Boscán's poem.

"Leandro y Hero" has three roughly equal sections, each created by the particular source material. After a nineteen-line preamble, there is a one-thousand-and-one-hundred-line part, which describes the initial meeting of Hero and Leander (about five hundred lines) and the declaration of their love (about six hundred lines). The action occurs within the space of one day. The main source is Musaeus, to whose argument Boscán adds an extensive psychological study of the hapless lovers. The second part is approximately eight hundred twenty-five lines and is an episodic interlude in the main action. It has three symmetrical parts: a three-hundred-line section treating Aristaeus' complaint to his mother Cyrene about the destruction of his beehives and Cyrene's advice to wrest from Proteus the secret of how to appease the gods; the one-hundred-sixty-line relation by Proteus of the story of Orpheus and Eurydice; and a three-hundred-fifty-line section describing Proteus' complaint to Neptune that everyone knows how to exact his secrets from him and Neptune's decision to establish one day a year for Proteus to reveal his prophesies to the Greeks. The first two sections come from Virgil's fourth *Georgics,* and the last event

appears to be Boscán's invention. The third part of the epic is
approximately eight hundred fifty lines long; it details the con-
summation of the lovers' desire and their subsequent death. It
comes structurally from Musaeus, but it is embellished and heavily
sentimentalized by paraphrases from Ovid.[2] The action of this last
part takes place on two nights divided by a period of two months
(the middle two hundred twenty-five lines of the section), during
which time winter storms separate the lovers.

The preamble to "Leandro y Hero" imitates the typical epic
mode by addressing through apostrophe the proper muse:

> Canta con voz suave y dolorosa,
> ¡o Musa! los amores lastimeros,
> que en suave dolor fueron criados.
> Canta también la triste mar en medio,
> y a Sesto de una parte, y de otra Abido,
> y amor acá y allá yendo y viniendo;
> y aquella diligente lumbrecilla,
> testigo fiel y dulce mensagera
> de dos fieles y dulces amadores.
> ¡O mereciente luz de ser estrella
> luciente y principal en las estrellas
> que fueron desde acá al cielo enviadas,
> y alcanzaron allá notables nombres!
> Pero comienza ya de cantar, Musa,
> el proceso y el fin destos amantes:
> el mirar, el hablar, el entenderse;
> el ir del uno, el esperar del otro,
> el desear y el acudir conforme,
> la lumbre muerta y a Leandro muerto.   (pp. 289–90)

> (Sing with soft and dolorous voice,
> oh Muse, the sad loves,
> that in soft dolor were nurtured.
> Sing also the sad sea between them,
> and Sestos on one side, and on the other Abydos,
> and love here and there going and coming;
> and that diligent little light,
> faithful witness and sweet messenger
> of two faithful and sweet lovers.
> Oh light meritorious of being a star
> shining and of first magnitude among the stars
> that were sent from here to heaven,

and achieved there notable names!
But begin now to sing, Muse,
the process and the end of these lovers:
the gazes, the speeches, the silent understanding;
the going of one, the waiting of the other,
correspondent desiring and succoring,
the dead light and dead Leander.)

The devices used in this passage to instill the blank verse with a poetic effect are characteristic for the entire poem. The stress usually falls on the sixth syllable, as in consonantal rhyme, but not always. Boscán depends more on the repetition of words and vowels and on parallelisms and bimembrations. In the first three verses, for example, the poet uses "suave y dolorosa" in the first line and repeats them as "suave dolor" in the third verse. He thus can place the invoked subject and object in the middle line ("¡O Musa! los amores lastimeros"), forming thereby a balance between the two repeated phrases.

For the next three lines Boscán again begins with "Canta" and, after placing "también la triste mar *en medio*" with its melancholic *m* alliteration, follows with a bimembrated and then a double bimembrated verse:

> *y* a Sesto de una parte, / *y* de otra Abido,
> *y* Amor acá *y* allá / *y*endo *y* viniendo.

The symmetry of the verses could not be more perfect. The sense of the sea separating the two lovers is solidly established by this separation of the lines into equal parts; and the use of the adjectives "lastimeros" and "triste" with the two direct objects points to the tragic substance of the epic. There is definitely a back-and-forth rhythm that imitates the going and coming of the hero across the Hellespont.

The subsequent lines employ both bimembration and the repetition of words by placing "fiel y dulce" and "fieles y dulces" in the exact center of two continuous verses. Boscán ties these first lines to the end of his poem, moreover, by repeating them in the final stanza: "Y en este mismo punto un torbellino / acabó de matar la lumbrecilla, testigo fiel y dulce mensagera / destos fieles y dulces amadores" (p. 376). The accent falls on the *u* in "dulce," and to connect it with the next line Boscán places "luz" in the sixth syllable position to continue the *u* rhyme. The next three lines use the same technique by placing an accented *a* in the central position: "principál," "acá," "allá." Thus, although there is no end-rhyme, an assonantal rhyme of the major stress carries the rhythm of the verses.

For the last six lines of the preamble, the poet again invokes the epic muse, then bimembrates and trimembrates the final lines to form a brilliantly conceived harmony of sound and meaning:

> *El* proceso / *y* / *el* fin [destos amantes]:
> *el* mirar, / *el* hablar, / *el* entenderse;
> *el* ir del uno, / *el* esperar del otro,
> *el* desear / *y* / *el* acudir [conforme],
> la lumbre muerta / *y* / a Leandro muerto.

The abundant repetition of *el* and *y*, the verbal separation of one lover from the other, the double use of "muerte" in the last line with the employment of "lumbre" (which sounds similar to Leandro) as a metaphor for Hero as well as a direct reference to the damsel's lamp, all create a magnificently balanced format that describes the tragic separation of the lovers.

The body of the poem begins on the same dichotomous note that characterizes the preamble. Boscán explains that Sestos and Abydos are two villages on each side of the Hellespont, one in Europe, the other in Asia, separated by the sea. Love stung with its arrows two inhabitants of these two villages:

> Era Leandro el dél, y el della Hero,
> iguales en linage y en hacienda,
> en valor, en saber y en hermosura.
> El estaba en Abido, y ella en Sesto.   (p. 290)

> (Leander was his name, and hers was Hero,
> equal in lineage and in estate,
> in valor, in wisdom, and in beauty.
> He was in Abydos, and she in Sestos.)

Hero was a vestal virgin in the temple of Venus, and while she served in the temple or lived in the tower of her parents' house by the sea she was immune to love. On the festival day dedicated to Venus and Adonis the populace entered the temple to pray. All were amazed by Hero's beauty, which competed with the Graces, Leda, Danae, Briseis, and Helen. The one most struck by her loveliness was Leander, whom Amor chose to wound with its arrow. Hero espied the youth's ardorous glances and fell under their spell. When night descended, Leander returned to the temple and found his beloved alone in the darkness. He sat beside her, and after a long while dared to take her hand in his so as to declare his desire.

As has been stressed by many critics, this courtly encounter of Hero and Leander is substantially different from Musaeus' original poem. Otis H. Green has noted, for example, that "what Boscán endeavored to do was to convert Musaeus' priestess of Aphrodite into a Renaissance *dama,* and to bring the passion of both lovers into conformity with the code of Platonic love as set forth in Castiglione's *Il Cortegiano.*"[3] Reichenberger views the protagonists' attitudes in the same vein: "Boscán sought to bring it [i.e., Musaeus' poem] into accord with the prevailing standards of sentiment and ethics of his own time. Instead of pagan sensualism we find sentimentalism and Christian struggle against love. Secretiveness of love in Musaeus is replaced by the ethos of fidelity. Whatever ethical concepts are found in the original are developed, but its sensualism is subdued" ("Boscán and the Classics," pp. 104–5).

Hero thus quickly reprimanded Leander for his unlawful advances, explaining that her life and body were dedicated to the virgin, so could never possibly return his love without incurring the wrath of her parents and the townspeople. But Leander wisely responded that Venus was the goddess of love and would wish that one of her number should marry someone with whom the virgin had become enamored. If it were not thus, her son Cupid would not have wounded him with the golden arrow. Hero succumbs to these reasonings, and tells the youth her name and where she lives by the sea. Leander in turn promises to swim across the strait to see her, advising that she put a light in her window to guide him as the north star guides the sailors. She agrees to his plan and the two lovers part until their secret rendezvous. Leander returns to Abydos sick and melancholic with love to await the appointed signal; but ten days pass without the appearance of the lighted lamp.

Here, one third of the way through the poem, Boscán intentionally stops the action. "But perhaps some will want to know," he remarks, "attentive in reading all this history, where Hero went so she could not so quickly give her desired signal." "Yo lo diré si con placer me escuchan, / y me dan facultad que me divierta / un poco del propósito empezado" (p. 324): "I will relate it if you listen with pleasure, / and you give me liberty to depart / a little from the stated subject matter." The poet is thus fully conscious of the episodic nature of this second part of his epic; but he includes it because the artistic standards of the time required interpolated tales.

As A. G. Reichenberger has noted, a Renaissance audience expected diversions from the main plot and the critics demanded them: "The insertion of extraneous episodes is at least partly due, no doubt, to an urge to display erudition and skill in translation; and the choice of subject matter, the nucleus of which is the Orpheus and Eurydice story, manifests once more Boscán's preference for the somber aspects of love, prevalent in his own lyrical output (the Orpheus and Eurydice myth could almost be called a sentimental duplication of the Hero and Leander theme, since both end tragically). Boscán's practice, however, was recommended by contemporary poetic theory" ("Boscán and the Classics," pp. 103–4). To substantiate the last sentence, Reichenberger quotes the following from the *Poetics* of Marcus Hieronymous Vida: "Quod si longarum, cordi magis ampla viarum / Sunt spatia, angustis cum res tibi finibus arcta, / In longum trahito arte. Viae tibi mille trahendi."

This middle section has three distinct parts, each with different speakers. The teller of the tales within the tale is of course Boscán. It is he who sings the opening lines about how one Aristaeus incurred the wrath of the nymphs and lost all he had for a misdeed against Orpheus. The narrator does not tell us directly who this Aristaeus is, however; nor does he relate why the man forfeited all his possessions.

Two thirds of the section comes from Virgil's *Georgics*. Book IV is dedicated to the cultivation of bees, and the first three hundred lines describe the value of bees and their maintenance. On line 315 Virgil stops his discussion of bees, in much the same way Boscán interrupted his epic of Leander and Hero, to relate who invented the art of creating bees spontaneously from a calf's putrified carcass. Virgil forthwith tells the legend of the shepherd Aristaeus who lost his bees to sickness and went to his mother Cyrene the water nymph to complain.

Boscán will follow Virgil's tale line by line, explaining how votive offerings were made and how Aristaeus was advised to go to Proteus' cave to bind the sea god and wrest the reason for the bees' loss from him. In Boscán's rendition, Aristaeus goes to the grand lake where his mother lives and delivers his complaint. Why did she and Apollo conceive him, he asks, if they were later to abandon him to suffer at the hands of the fates. His mother hears him and leaves the companionship of the many nymphs to conduct her son to the altar of Ocean, where they make a sacrifice to appease him. With the good omen confirmed, Cyrene speaks to her son and tells him how he must go to the cave of Proteus and tie up the old sea god until the things Aristaeus wants to know are revealed. Aristaeus dutifully goes to Proteus' abode and waits until the sea god enters and falls asleep. He then ties him up and, after witnessing the god undergo a thousand transformations to escape, he asks Proteus to restore to him the lost goods.

Proteus' response is the middle section of the episode; but instead of being an answer to Aristaeus, it is a one-hundred-fifty-line account of the Orpheus and Eurydice story. This part is also from Virgil's *Georgics*. The Mantuan has Proteus explain to Aristaeus that the loss of the bees was punishment for causing the death of Eurydice, for the girl was bitten by the serpent while fleeing from the shepherd's lustful advances. Boscán again copies almost line by line from Virgil the story of the ill-fated lovers, ending the account exactly as Virgil did with Orpheus' head floating down the river Hebrus still crying out for Eurydice. Virgil's poem ends after this narration with Proteus leaping into the sea and Cyrene advising her son to sacrifice four young bulls to Orpheus. Aristaeus follows her counsel, and on the ninth day discovers that swarms of bees have been born in the carcasses.

Boscán's rendition is as follows: Orpheus was so saddened that he wandered over the hills singing to his lost Eurydice. He even penetrated the kingdom of Pluto to free her from death. He left Hades with Eurydice behind him, as Proserpina had required; but as they neared the end of the journey the musician turned to see if Eurydice was indeed following him, and thus he lost her forever. Orpheus wept for seven months. He even rejected the attentions of the women of Thrace, who, angered at his disdain, attacked him during a nocturnal sacrifice to Bacchus and tore his body into a thousand pieces. Boscán opted to delete Virgil's last thirty lines, where Aristaeus appeases Orpheus and is given the secret of spontaneous propagation of bees.

The last part of the episode is Proteus' harangue before Neptune that everyone has learned how to make him reveal his secrets. The exact source for this section has not been found. After relating the Orpheus and Eurydice story to Aristaeus, the sea god throws himself into the water and swims to the palace of Neptune, where he delivers his plea. He tells Neptune that he is tired of having so many people tie him up to make him reveal his secrets; and the worst part is that they want to know such silly things as why their bees died. Proteus therefore does not want the gift of prophecy any more, since he never has a day's rest because of it. The gods are saddened at the infamous way Proteus has been treated, and Ocean rises to offer a solution. He recommends that one day of the year be set aside when the populace can come to Proteus and ask that he reveal his secrets. Everyone agrees, and the festival day for the prophecies is set. It is to this festival that Hero has gone after her initial meeting, and she was delayed ten days because the trip was three days each way and the festival lasted four days. In this way Boscán connects the episode to the main story.

Thematic relationships between this section and the history of Leander and Hero are at best tenuous. The tale of Orpheus and Eurydice has a tragic finale similar to the end that awaits Hero and her lover. Proteus is a sea god, as are Neptune and Ocean; and it is the sea that separates Hero and Leander. Aristaeus is the son of the sea nymph Cyrene, who aids him achieve his goal; and the nymph Doris and her daughters help Leander cross the Hellespont. None of these analogies is important enough to include such a long episode, however; so it must be assumed that Boscán had no direct relation in mind between the two tales, but included the extraneous material principally as a diversion for the reader. A. G. Reichenberger faced this same problem of internal coherence among the parts and resolved nothing. He did give a rational explanation for the extended speeches of Proteus and Ocean before Neptune:

It should be noted also that the long discourses of Proteus and Oceanus, although verbose and lengthy, are well constructed, with introduction, main part, and conclusion clearly discernible in each. These orations remind us of the speeches which the classical historians inserted in their works, observing in them the rules of rhetorical theory. No direct source has been ascertained for the subject matter of the episode and it might very well be Boscán's own invention. Just as he added the Virgilian matter, Boscán offered a council of gods and long speeches, motivated by his desire to adorn the original story with as many features found in classical literature as he felt compatible with it. ("Boscán and the Classics," p. 111)

The main story begins again precisely where it left off. As soon as Hero returns to Sestos, she puts the lamp in the window. Her lover espies the light, delivers a harangue to steel his heart against the danger, and declares to the waters the famous last verse from Martial's epigram ("Parcite dum propero; mergite, dum redeo"): "¡Mientras que voy, o aguas, amansáos! / ¡Ahogáme después quando volviere!" (p. 356). He dives into the sea and with the aid of Doris and her nymphs, crosses over to Sestos. The love scene takes place after the two swear to marriage bonds; and the sexual encounter is, according to Reichenberger, "a less passionate version in which the lady (*señora*) is put on a high pedestal, adored by the lowly lover in the tradition of the *cancioneros* and the troubadours" ("Boscán and the Classics," p. 107).

The two lovers part after their first night of love with little hope of meeting again for a long time, since the winter season has begun and high winds make crossing the sea difficult. Throughout the long months of November and December the two lovers wait and watch to see if the sea will become calm. The poet, meanwhile, describes in detail the mental dispositions of the two lovers as they suffer each other's absence. The seas finally subside and Leander watches with anticipation for the signal from Hero's tower. The girl lights her lamp, but the wind blows it out. She lights it again, and again, until it burns brightly. Leander, on the other shore, invokes "Santa Venus" (p. 371) and begins his journey. When he gets halfway across, however, a strong wind springs up. The youth struggles to stay afloat and to keep his lover's lamp in sight; but a high wave covers him, and his lifeless body is tossed on the beach below Hero's tower. She looks from her window and by the first rays of dawn espies her lover on the sand:

> Entonces, con la rabia de la muerte,
> a rasgar empezó sus vestiduras,
> mesando sus cabellos y arañando
> su lindo rostro, sus hermosos pechos,
> hinchiendo de aullidos todo el campo.

Tras esto, así sin más pensar su muerte,
dexándose caer de la ventana,
dió sobre el cuerpo muerto de Leandro,
que aun entonces se le acababa el mundo.
Y así se fueron juntas las dos almas
a los campos Elisios para siempre.   (p. 376)

(Then, with the rage of death,
she began to tear her clothes,
pulling out her hair and scratching
her beautiful face, her beautiful breasts,
filling with howls the countryside.
After this, without thinking once about death,
letting herself fall from the window,
she landed on the dead body of Leander,
and in that moment left this world.
And thus the two souls went together
to the Elysian fields forever.)

Thus ends the first short epic in Spain of classical subject matter and one of the best examples of blank verse in Spanish literature. As Otis Green has indicated, the tragic finale does not deny Christian sentiments on Boscán's part: "Neither this act of suicide, nor Boscán's concern with Platonic and Stoic concepts, can be regarded as pointing toward non-Christian tendencies in Boscán's thinking or feeling, as a complete study of Boscán will show. Greek and Roman ethics and moral wisdom were regarded, both by Boscán and by Castiglione, as aid and handmaidens of Christian morality" ("Boscán," p. 140). Green's justification for this statement is the heavy Neoplatonic ambience of "Leandro y Hero," which Boscán absorbed from Castiglione's *Il cortegiano*. Green's best example is the description of Hero, who is described as "a perfect type of Renaissance *temperancia*, of Stoic *virtus*, and of Platonic harmony" (p. 134). Musaeus, according to Green, described Hero's beauty and its effect on the men of Sestos in purely physical terms; but Boscán described Hero's body as exemplifying the soul it covered and thus he associated admiration of her beauty with contemplation of the highest good of the soul (p. 135).

A. G. Reichenberger comes to much the same conclusions about Boscán's poem:

Boscán tries to create a classical atmosphere by imitating the more easily imitable features of classical poetry, mainly embellishing his work with mythological lore. But what we feel today as typically Hellenic in Musaeus, the straightforwardness, the simple plastic force of Musaeus' language, together with his sensualism of Hellenistic heritage, have not been carried over into Boscán's Castilian version. In compensation, Boscán sentimentalizes Musaeus' tersely told epic with psychological analyses in the style of the Ovidian *Heroides*. However, sentiments expressed in this Ovidian style of feeling are no longer those of a pagan priestess of Venus, but those of a Christian Renaissance lady. Glimpses of contemporary Spanish life and concepts are anachronistically evident here and there in the ancient story. ("Boscán and the Classics," p. 117)

While Reichenberger's summary is in general valid, it would nevertheless be unfair to Boscán to condemn him for being a Renaissance man rather than a Greek. Boscán is just as bound to his milieu as were Musaeus and Ovid; and it would be fallacious to think that his poetry should not exhibit Christian morality, courtly sentimentalism, and Spanish culture.

What surprises the reader about "Leandro y Hero," in fact, is the high level of objectivity and the lack of a moral ending, two things that are difficult to find in any Spanish writer before Boscán. The ending of the poem, for example, is so straightforward as to appear truncated. The poet neither sentimentalizes nor personalizes Hero's death, nor does he attempt to fabricate a didactic lesson from it. Hero, and Leander as well, simply dies. There is no outside influence nor is there any particular reason for either of the lovers' deaths, except perhaps youthful rashness. This attitude on the poet's part, while it is not anti-Christian, is clearly non-Christian, and marks the decisive breach between the authoritative medieval God-centered universe and the empirical Renaissance man-centered world.

II   *"Chapter I"*

Entitled simply "Capítulo I," this three-hundred-eighty-five-line epistolary poem is one of the first examples of the Italian *terza rima* in Spain, preceded only by the elegies and second eclogue of Garcilaso de la Vega and Boscán's "Epístola." "Chapter I" imitates the popular Italian *Capitoli,* and describes the poet's request to serve his "señora" in Love's court: "El alma mía / se echa a tus

pies, merced te demando, / para poder servirte noche y día"
(p.377). The lover reminds her that he has spent all of his time
adoring her; and he begs in a very courtly manner that she remake
his tortured soul by accepting his service, for thus she would be
giving life instead of causing death. Look into my heart, he asks
her, and you will see how my whole life has been dedicated to
worshiping you. The poet remembers all too well the day and the
hour that he first saw her. He at first hesitated, wanting to love her
with all his heart, but fearing at the same time a rebuttal. His amorous thoughts won the day, and he began officially to serve her. He
accepted every opportunity to be in her presence, and once even
hoped to tell her of his sufferings; but he was timorous of her reac-
tion. When he finally did announce his love to her, she responded
kindly and did not become angry or rebuff him (as all the past
ladies did in the courtly affairs).

The initial acceptance by his lady gave Boscán the opportunity to
enjoy her presence and to contemplate her body inch by inch: "Tu
cuerpo letra a letra le leía, / aunque miralle particularmente / mi
seso pocas veces lo sufría" (pp. 381–82). From there Boscán undertook the contemplation of her soul: "Parecía que el alma andaba
hurtando, / ora una vista y otra dende un rato, / de su necesidad se
aprovechando" (p. 382). With the soul's contemplation, moreover,
his adoration underwent a radical change ("trataba Amor conmigo
un nuevo trato," p. 382), for the poet now beheld in his lady the
whole of Nature summarized and projected:

> El cielo acá en el mundo te dispuso
> con obra tal, que al tiempo que te hizo,
> el bien que en él pusieron, en tí puso.
> Natura en tu labor se satisfizo;
> ....
> Quanto bien entendemos, está junto
> en tu espíritu, del cual su rayo estiende
> en tu cuerpo su luz de punto en punto.
> Y por aquí también su llama enciende
> aquel ardiente fuego, que consume
> todo el mal en el alma do se aprende.
> ....
> Por tí nuestro entender tiene esperanza
> de levantarse al movedor primero,
> de una en otra y en otra semejanza. (pp. 382–83)

(The Heavens here on the earth made you
with such art, that at the same time they made you,
the good that they put in it was put in you.
Nature outdid itself in your creation;
....
All we understand as good is joined
in your spirit, from which rays extend
their light throughout your body.
And from here also its flame kindles
that ardent fire that consumes
all the evil that exists in my soul.
....
Because of you our understanding is hopeful
of ascending to the Prime Mover,
from one resemblance to another and to another.)

Boscán could have received this material from any number of contemporary sources, since Neoplatonism was by 1535 part of the
Italian *Weltansicht*. His major source was certainly Castiglione's *Il
cortegiano,* whose Fourth Book describes in minute detail the Platonic system of love as an ascent from the physical to the spiritual,
from the terrestrial to the celestial, from the visible to the invisible.
The ascent is made, as Boscán notes, by rising from one
"semejanza" to another. The normal equivalent for this term in
English is "semblance" or "resemblance"; yet what Boscán means
is something more like "analogy." The understanding moves from
one level of reality to another higher one by recognizing the
analogical similarity between the higher — and therefore more
desirable — level and the lower position; for the difference between
any two levels is that the upper one has a higher proportion of
divine goodness. The participant in the Platonic ascent repeats this
comparison of analogical spheres, always opting to ascend to the
next level, until he reaches the uppermost station, which is the contemplation of divine beauty.

In *Il cortegiano,* the proponent of this system is Pietro Bembo
(1470–1547), the famous poet and linguist who, interestingly, corrected the proofs of the *Cortegiano* because Castiglione was in
Spain at the time. Bembo describes the ascent as one that begins
with the courtier's recognition that rational love is happier than
sensual love because it does not disturb the spirit or the body. From
this stage the lover must come to realize that a universal concept of
all bodies is necessarily more worthy of contemplation than the

loveliness of his lady's particular body, for the former participates more in the universal idea of what a beautiful woman should be like. But the courtier must not stop here; he should turn now within himself in order to contemplate that general beauty seen only by the eyes of the mind, for if a composite of all physical beauties is lovely, consider how adorable will be the abstract conception of beauty. This level is not the final one, however; for, in Bembo's words:

Just as from the particular beauty of one body it guides the soul to the universal beauty of all bodies, so in the highest stage of perfection beauty guides it from the particular intellect to the universal intellect. Hence, the soul, aflame with the most holy fire of true divine love, flies to unite itself with the angelic nature; and not only completely abandons the senses, but has no longer any need of reason's discourse; for, transformed into an angel, it understands all things intelligible, and without any veil or cloud views the wide sea of pure divine beauty, and receives it into itself, enjoying that supreme happiness of which the senses are incapable.[4]

It is this same Platonic scale that will become the mystic ladder to spiritual perfection in the post-Tridentine writings of San Juan de la Cruz and Fray Luis de Leon.

Although Boscán recognizes these theoretical heights to which his thoughts rise when he contemplates his lady's soul, he still admits a great amount of suffering and torment. In this instance, however, the pain brings a delicate finesse to his love that makes everything worthwhile: "Digo que amor me llega a tal fineza, / que granjeo mi mal y le regalo, / y me alivio con él en mi tristeza" (p. 383). This "fineza" is the courtly refinement that comes with a proper control of passion; so Boscán still has his feet in both amorous worlds. The poet defines this finesse as loving, serving, obeying, being of value to his lady, and bettering himself: "Mi bien y mi descanso es regalarme / en amarte, servirte, obedecerte, / en valer para tí y en mejorarme" (p.384). For this reason he cannot possibly live outside of her service.

There is only one resentment the lover therefore has of his beloved, and that is jealousy. This disease bothers him terribly, and to alleviate it he is going to tell a story to his lady. The tale relates the events surrounding the death of Iphigenia: the contrary winds that held back the Greek fleet at Aulos, the revelation that they had to sacrifice a virgin, and the cruel murder of Iphigenia by her own father Agamemnon. Many poets and painters, continues Boscán, gained fame depicting that sad event. One painting in particular was famous, for it presented excellently the suffering of the family. The brothers were presented weeping and the mother senseless in the arms of her serving girls. To show even greater sorrow, the painter depicted the father with a cape over his head.[5] If the poet wishes also to describe his pain, he will have to be as dextrous as that painter. The pain his love creates is similar to that of the mother, but jealousy causes him even more torment than that which the father suffers, so in his painting he will depict himself stretched out dead: "Y harto mostraré lo que dél siento, / mostrándome por él tendido y muerto" (p. 389). And with that statement he abruptly ends the poem.

The differences between this work and the courtly poetry of Boscán's early period are remarkably clear. The tone here is much lighter, and the style is looser and not as cramped. There are classical references to Greek literature (as opposed to Roman or Italian), and there is an emphasis on jealousy, a disease that did not preoccupy the courtly lover because all obstacles, even rivals, were considered necessary to the refinement of love. "Chapter I" is thus a later piece, but it still does not possess the full-bodied Renaissance spirit that has been seen in "Leander and Hero" and that will appear again in "Octava rima," to which "Chapter I" is similar in the use of a classical anecdote to illustrate a point.

III   *"Epistle"*

The three-hundred-forty-seven-line "Epístola" in *terza rima* that follows "Capítulo I" in Book Three definitely belongs to an earlier period in which Boscán was still writing courtly poetry of unrequited love. Here, the poet sends his letter to a lady who has continually rejected his advances. The piece is thus charged with the early vocabulary of "morir," "dolor," "tristeza," "tormento," "mal," etc. The poem begins:

> El que sin tí vivir ya no querría,
> y ha mucho tiempo que morir desea,
> por ver si tanto mal se acabaría,
> a tu merced suplica que ésta lea.   (p. 393)

(He who without you would not want to live,
and who has desired to die for a long time now,
to see if so much misfortune could end,
supplicates Your Mercy to read this.)

Boscán then pours out his pain to his lady, explaining that he does
not know any longer in what other way he can serve her. His will
therefore turns to his pain for support, and finds only sadness.
Since his lady will not satisfy him in any of this, perhaps she will at
least listen to his complaints; for even such a little favor as that will
alleviate somewhat his suffering. Assuredly, he continues, she will
consider them infantile; but does she think it is childish to be sad,
to have honor and soul in danger, to have the understanding
destroyed, and to suffer a thousand scornings and rebuttals? It is
these "niñerías" that will finally kill him if she continues to wound
him so harshly.

Boscán then changes the course of the poem to declare that he
should actually not complain if his lady rejects him, for she is so
perfect that nothing she does could be wrong. Perhaps he should
not love her then, since it bothers her; but who could not help
loving a person of such grace and beauty? He sees no remedy to the
situation, since the more he declares his love the more he angers
her. Nevertheless, he will continue to adore her: "No plega a Dios
que quiera yo enojarte, / ni te quiera un punto ser pesado, / mas
mucho menos quiero desamarte" (p. 397). He explains that his
"crudo amor," as does all courtly love, increases with impossibili-
ties and rejections to where the pain becomes unbearable. So from
this "mal fiero," as he properly terms it, he expects only death,
unless she fortifies him with recognition of his service. He finally
declares that he is coming to visit her, although seeing her may kill
him.

The whole epistle could not be more medieval. It is probably the
first poem in which Boscán used *terza rima,* perhaps as early as
1526 when Navagiero first urged him to try the new meters, and
therefore it has a certain historical value as the earliest example of
the verse form in Spanish; but the tone, language, and style still
belong to the era of the *coplas* and the early sonnets.

IV *"Epistle to don Diego de Mendoza"*

The publication of Juan Boscán's and Garcilaso de la Vega's works in 1543 presented to the Hispanic world the first three verse epistles in Spanish. The earliest piece is Garcilaso's "Epístola a Boscán," written in blank verse on October 12, 1534. It is modeled on the epistles of Quintus Horatius Flaccus (65-8 B.C.),[6] and it broke with the contemporary Italian epistles, written in *terza rima,* in its use of blank verse. As Elias L. Rivers has noted: "We can at least conclude that being a thorough humanist even by Italian standards, for he himself wrote poems in classical Latin, Garcilaso deliberately chose blank verse as the most acceptable modern equivalent of dactylic hexameter; he seems to have considered it more in keeping than terza rima with the informality of an epistle written to a friend."[7]

The second epistle is a poem in *terza rima* from don Diego Hurtado de Mendoza to Boscán, written about 1539. It is inserted in Book Two immediately before Boscán's reply, which is the third example in the volume and is thought to have been composed in late 1539 or early 1540. The latter two epistles follow the Horatian paradigm more closely than Garcilaso's does, although they are both written in tercets rather than in blank verse.

Garcilaso's poem does not imitate any particular epistle by Horace, although it does have close formal resemblances with the Roman poet's briefer, wittier, and more personal letters. Furthermore, the use of tercets allies Boscán and Mendoza with the Italian epistolary tradition initiated at the close of the Middle Ages by Petrarch, who rediscovered Horace and wrote *Epistulae metricae* in imitation of his epistles. Coluccio Salutati and other Italian humanists continued to spread the influence of the Roman bard; and commentaries were done by Landino, Poliziano, and others. Both Boscán and Mendoza would have been thoroughly familiar with this literary tradition. Rivers observes: "Mendoza and Boscán, with their more explicit and doctrinal Horatianism, were probably more directly indebted than Garcilaso to the precedents set by the Italian humanists; certainly this is true of their choice of *terza rima* rather than blank verse. And their more elaborate verse form is indicative of a generally more elevated style: their relatively infrequent use of colloquialisms and their more predominantly impersonal tone of moralizing generality stand in contrast to the friendly directness of Garcilaso's unrhymed epistle" ("Horatian Epistle," p. 190). The format the Spaniards followed came from Horace's *Epistulae,* a poetic form the Roman invented and perfected. Its basic function was to discourse in an informal manner on some moral topic. "Except when very brief and held to the demands of the situation," writes Smith Palmer Bovie, translator and editor of Horace's epistles, "they are discursive literary reflections, 'essays.' It has been said that what makes a letter an epistle is the predominance of general content over topical interest and that these poems were not so much letters, written on the stated occasion to the person in question, as compositions born of *l'esprit d'escalier* and aimed generally at a cultivated audience."[8] The epistolary format of the poems comes from the philosophical epistles in prose by the Greeks and the early Romans, especially Epicurus, who seems to be the major influence on Horace. The name of the person addressed is invariably in the first line, and some personal data accompany the name. This personal note usually reappears at the end of the epistle. The philosophical subject matter of the middle section is what differentiates the epistle from the normal letter, and it is what will become the sole purpose of the Horatian epistles of Francisco de Aldana, Rodrigo Caro, Juan Rufo, Andrés Fernández de Andrada, and others.

The catalyst for Boscán's epistolary effort is the poem by Diego Hurtado de Mendoza (1504–75). This "perfect courtier" was the author of the valuable *Guerra de Granada* (published posthumously in 1627), ambassador to Venice and Rome for Charles the Fifth, and an accomplished poet (his poetry was not published until 1610, by Frey Juan Diaz Hidalgo). Mendoza is also thought by many to be the author of *Lazarillo de Tormes.*[9]

Mendoza's epistle begins with a direct quote from Horace's Epistle I.6 ("Nil admirari prope res est una, Numici, / solaque quae possit facere et servare beatum"):

> El no maravillarse hombre de nada,
> me parece, Boscán, ser una cosa
> que basta a darnos vida descansada.   (p. 402)

> (For a man not to marvel at anything,
> seems to me, Boscán, to be something
> that suffices to give us a tranquil life.)

Mendoza then applies this ethic to the heavens, the earth and its hidden treasures, the ambitious courtier, the favorite, and the aspiring scholar. This world, he explains, treats us as aliens; and the other world hides its secrets from us, so there is no reason to desire nor to fear anything. There are many things to admire, such as red bronze, marble, fame, silks, emeralds, pearls, rubies, diamonds, beautiful women, Boscán's own poetic ability, the fortunate farmer; yet these things come and go.

The poet now shifts from the *Nil admirari* theme to the new motif of Stoic *Virtus* by declaring that virtue is the best arm against the world's folly: "Si te puede sacar desta contienda / la virtud, como viene sola y pura, / al resto del deleyte ten la rienda" (p. 403). The introduction of virtue by Mendoza begins a long section dedicated to the Stoic negative, where the poet lists what Boscán should avoid. Poisoned arrows, gunfire, battles, war, the sea, storms, earthquakes, none of these things move the good and just man. Neither fame nor a long life nor personal ambition should affect one's career. The good and just man sees all objectively and is satisfied with the life he has, thereby putting no trust in anything subject to change. He mixes the harsh with the bland, the bitter with the sweet, and pleasure with severity. This ability is the height of happiness, for it leads to the golden mean, the *Aurea mediocritas,* or, as Mendoza terms it, "medianeza comedida" (p. 407). Its characteristics are precisely defined by the Spaniard:

> En qualquier medio vive satisfecho;
> procura de ordenar, en quanto puede,
> que en todo la razón venza el provecho.
> Esto no sigue tanto que él no quede
> dulce en humano trato y conversable,
> ni dé a entender al mundo que le hiede.
> Pónese en el estado razonable;
> nunca espera, ni teme, ni se cura
> de lo que le parece que es mudable.   (p. 406)

> (With any mean he lives satisfied;
> he procures to order, as well as he can,
> that in everything reason should conquer expediency.
> From this it does not follow that he not remain
> kind in conversation and human treatment,
> nor should he fall into treating the world as if it stank.

He should put himself in a reasonable state;
he should never hope, nor fear, nor worry
about what he considers to be mutable.)

The role of the Stoic *Recto ratio* is clear. Although Mendoza could
have received these ideas from Horace or any of the numerous
commentators on the Roman thinkers, Mendoza probably got the
material directly from Seneca's *De vita beata,* where he would have
read that "the highest good is a mind that scorns the happenings of
chance, and rejoices in virtue," and that "it is the power of the
mind to be unconquerable, wise from experience, calm in action,
showing the while much courtesy and consideration in intercourse
with others," and "that the happy man is one who is freed from
both fear and desire because of the gift of reason."[10]
   If Mendoza led this life ordered by reason, the poet explains of
himself, he would have a delicious existence, free of governmental
worries and endless hopes. He would live a rustic course of life —
here begins the famous *Beatus ille* theme — with simple food, old
wine, and clear water. He would lead his flocks to pasture, feed his
oxen, act as judge for the laborers, listen to their stories, songs, and
proverbs. Bosán and Jerónimo Agustín, Durall, Monleón, and
Cetina would come to visit him. And if only Marfira could be
present, for whom his heart pines! Mendoza now directs his epistle
to this lady and asks her to listen to the sweet songs of the birds in
the countryside, to smell the odor of the fields, to see the clear
rivers, and to taste the fruit of the trees. There in the country the
problems of government would be of no concern.
   After this impassioned Petrarchan apostrophe to Marfira,
which, as E. Rivers has pointed out, "is irreconcilably opposed in
spirit to Mendoza's earlier dictum of 'nil admirari'" ("Horatian
Epistle," p. 191), the poet directs himself again to Boscán to terminate the poem on the Stoic note of a life in the country adjusted
to the golden mean:

   Yo, Boscán, no procuro otro tesoro
   sino poder vivir medianamente,
   ni escondo otra riqueza, ni otra adoro.
   Si aquí hallas algún inconveniente,
   como hombre diestro y no como yo soy,
   me desengaña dello incontinente,
   y si no, ven conmigo adonde voy.   (p. 410)

(I, Boscán, procure no other treasure
than to be able to live moderately,
nor do I hide any other treasure, nor do I adore any other.
If you find here something inconvenient,
for an upright man and not as I am,
undeceive me about it immediately,
and if not, come to where I am.)

Mendoza's epistle is thus structured around four classic topoi: *Nil admirari, Virtus, Aurea mediocritas,* and *Beatus ille.* They are introduced in that order and each one merges with and is the basic cause for the next topos. If you learn not to marvel at anything, lectures Mendoza, you will achieve virtue, which will instill in your life a golden mean regulated by right reason; and the only place to cultivate this beatitude is in the country, away from the denigrating influence of the court. Juan Boscán picks up all four of these themes in his reply to Don Diego, but he manipulates them to map a new and more humanistically wholesome road to happiness.

A. G. Reichenberger has noted a number of other similarities: "The *Epístolas* show great similarity in structure. Both take up the *Nil admirari* and the *Beatus ille* theme in the same order, both speak of love in the country, both give glimpses of their authors' personality, although the autobiographical element is much more striking in Boscán than in the epistle of his friend. Mendoza paraphrases Horace's *Nil admirari* epistle quite faithfully, using the first half of it almost completely and at least two passages from the second part. It would seem that Mendoza emphasizes the *Aurea mediocritas* concept somewhat more strongly than Boscán, and there is no Neo-Platonism in his poem."[11]

Boscán opens his epistle by remarking that the friend's letter has caused him to write verses again after he had quite forgotten how to do it, and he hopes that Mendoza's style will improve his own. Boscán then gives his opinion of Mendoza's *Nil admirari* philosophy:

> Digo también que el no maravillarse
> es propio de juicio bien compuesto.
> Quien sabe y quiere a la virtud llegarse,
> pues las cosas verá desde lo alto,
> nunca terná de qué pueda alterarse.   (pp. 411–12)

(I also say that to not marvel
is proper for a well composed mind.
He who knows and desires to reach virtue,
since he will see everything from on high,
never will have anything to be disturbed about.)

The new element introduced by Boscán that is totally lacking in Horace as well as in Mendoza's epistle is the phrase "pues las cosas verá desde lo alto." The poet elaborates the motif by remarking that the virtuous man can walk among the stars, free from conflict and surprises, without moving from where he is: "Todo lo alcanzará sin dar gran salto, / sin moverse andará por las estrellas, / seguro de alborozo y sobresalto" (p. 412). From up there he will see the beauties of the natural world and will confess their loveliness. But he will not stop there; rather he will rise up to the Mover of all things to contemplate the great secrets of the world's beauty: "Subirse ha al movedor de todas cosas, / y allí contemplará grandes secretos / hasta en las florecillas y en las rosas" (p. 412). There he will see the sun's course and its incredible velocity, the moon and the thousand other trajectories and paths of the seven planets. He will finally see more than we here could ever see; and, returning now to his principle idea, he will thus never marvel at these things: "Y en maravillas no maravillado, / estrará sin sentir jamás estremos" (p. 412).

This height to which the virtuous man rises is of course the Neoplatonic world of ideas. The sage rises above the world of shadows and images to exist in the real world of objects. It is the same hierarchy that Plato applied to love in the *Symposium* and that Bembo, by way of Plotinus and Marcilio Ficino, paraphrased in *Il cortegiano*. Plato explained it in a different way in the allegory of the cave in Book VII of the *Republic,* where man's existence was compared to being chained in a dark cave in which the only reality was the reflection of objects on a wall. The wise man, however, frees himself and ascends to the daylight, where slowly but surely he accustoms his sight to see the objects as they really are. The most famous Spanish exponent of this Platonic ladder is Fray Luis de Leon in his Horatian odes "Morada del cielo," "Noche serena," and "Oda a Francisco Salinas."

Another major difference between Horace's and Mendoza's *Nil admirari* philosophy on the one hand and Boscán's rendition on the other has been described by A. G. Reichenberger: "In Boscán's rendering of the Horatian thought we note an important shift of emphasis. For Horace, the *Nil admirari,* the Latin version of the Stoic-Epicurian *ataraxia,* is the only means of attaining happiness, goal of all philosophy. Boscán, in saying that *el no maravillarse* is the essential trait of *de juicio bien compuesto,* uses an aesthetic term. *Bien compuesto* means beauty through equilibrium and order." Reichenberger thus concludes that "the Horatian general philosophic motto assumes in Boscán an aesthetic quality which is essentially aristocratic" ("Boscán's *Epístola a Mendoza,*" p. 4). The "well composed" idea naturally concurs also with the prevailing Renaissance notions of beauty deriving principally from harmony of the parts, the right proportions, symmetry, and equilibrium.

Boscán continues to describe this false world as seen by the observer from the heights of that real world. The virtuous man will see our strengths as weaknesses, our delights as a waste of energy, our abundance as poverty. Men will appear as ants, and oaks as underbrush. He will be as the person who sees people dancing but does not hear the music and therefore knows the participants to be mad. He will laugh at our worries and hopes, and nothing will surprise him: "Las cosas para otros espantosas, / de nuevas o de grandes, no podrán / ser jamás para él maravillosas" (p. 413). Neither his own pain or anyone else's will concern him. This indeed, comments Boscán, will be the fortunate man! In Senecan terms, he will have ataraxia, that certain immurement from the effects of the passions, that imperturbability which characterizes the perfect sage.

At this point in the epistle, Boscán changes direction with three consecutive tercets that begin with "pero." Quite realistically, he admits that for most people the ascent of the spirit is more talk than deeds; in fact, here on this earth things are in such a state that the person with fewer vices is considered to be good. Moreover, Boscán does not seek any kind of extreme or harsh regimen: "No curemos de andar tras los estremos, / pues dellos huye la filosofía/ de los buenos autores que leemos" (p. 414). Rather than the rocky path set by Xenocrates he prefers the temperate way of Plato. This advice is a reaffirmation of the *Aurea mediocritas* advocated by Mendoza. Boscán comments four times on the necessity to "templar" our actions, concluding, as did Mendoza, that the middle

way is the surest road to virtue. In the very next line, however,
Boscán breaks with Mendoza's philosophy to follow a new and personal trajectory. He reports that in order to follow the golden mean
he has married and settled down to the family life:

> El estado mejor de los estados
> es alcanzar la buena medianía,
> con la qual se remedian los cuidados.
> Y así yo por seguir aquesta vía,
> heme casado con una muger,
> que es principio y fin del alma mía.   (p. 415)

> (The best state of all states
> is to achieve the good mean,
> with which all cares are remedied.
> And thus I, in order to follow that way,
> have married a woman,
> who is the alpha and omega of my soul.)

This marriage has given his life a new meaning and a firm foundation, where inconstancy has ceased to be a problem. All those
things that used to be burdens or torments — the lover's complaints, the sex act, bad food — have been annulled by the wholesome love of marriage, which is the same "casto amor, que Dios
del cielo envía" that Boscán praised so highly in Sonnet XC.

After the mention of his marriage, the poet immediately introduces the *Beatus ille* theme that Mendoza utilized so well: "Así que
yo ni quiero ya, ni puedo / tratar sino de vida descansada, / sin
colgar de esperanza ni de miedo" (p.416). Boscán's "vida descansada" is elaborated, according to Reichenberger, along three main
lines: "1) the contrast between the peaceful contentment of country life and the ambitious restlessness of city life; 2) the description
of country life, praising the wholesome meals and the enjoyment of
unpretentious company; 3) love in the country, sitting under the
trees by the brook and reading the ancient poets" ("Boscán's *Epístola a Mendoza*," p. 8).

Included as the central motif in all of these topics is the *Ne quid
nimis*, nothing in excess. Boscán comments that he has no desire to
be wealthy, but he does not want to be impoverished either; nor
does he want to live continually in the country, but only to retire
there when he wearies of city life, and vice versa. He then describes

the simple routine of the village, where he and his wife will walk along the river bank talking of amorous delights, and perhaps even making love under some green beech tree. They will take along some books, such as the *Aeneid,* the *Iliad,* the *Odyssey,* Propertius, and Catullus. He will think upon his past errors, and rejoice that he is free of love's madness. He and his wife will return to their cottage at nightfall to eat a simple and wholesome meal; then they will enjoy the peace of the evening until it is time to go to bed. At this point Boscán interjects the only lightly erotic note in the entire corpus of his poetry: "What from this time until morning / may transpire, let it pass now without being told, / since my pen does not care to be frivolous" (p. 422).

Boscán closes his letter with the mention of the same friends that Mendoza applauded. When he and Doña Ana tire of the country, he remarks, they will return to town to be with Mosén Durall, Jerónimo Agustín and Monleón. But, concludes the poet, it is time to close so that there will be something to write about in the next letter.

It is patent that the structure of Boscán's epistle is modelled on Mendoza's. Both works begin the *Nil admirari* topos, introduce next the *Virtus* theme, and give *Aurea mediocritas* as the way to virtue. Both letters then treat the *Beatus ille* topos as the place where the temperate life is best enjoyed, and both close with the mention of the same close friends who will participate in the idyllic existence. Thus, while Mendoza followed closely classical models and rarely strayed from their form and content, Boscán imitated Mendoza. For this reason the Catalan probably did not feel the pull of the *Imitatio Classici* so strongly, and added a number of elements neither present in Mendoza's epistle nor in the Latin models.

The most important literary addition is the Neoplatonic ascent through the spheres to the Prime Mover, which is totally absent in Mendoza's epistle as well as in all Spanish poets before Boscán. It gives his epistle the spiritual accent necessary to humanize the classical notion of the "vida descansada" with the Christian doctrine of serving God in every way. For a medieval mind, to retire to the country means to withdraw from all worldly pleasures, seeking a monastic life dedicated solely to serving God, including the necessary extremes of silence, abstinence, solitude, mortification of the flesh, and vigilance. For Mendoza and the Classics, to retire to the country means to flee the evils of city life, seeking the idyllic simplicities reminiscent of the Golden Age, where a virtuous soul is equivalent to freedom from pain and turmoil. For Boscán, to retire to the country means to leave behind the world of illusions to seek the spiritual world of realities, to remain in this world but to participate simultaneously in God's world. It is something that neither the hermit nor the classical Mendoza could achieve, because the former rejected the world and the latter fled from it, seeking only a state of ataraxia, after which one would attain virtue. Mendoza therefore preached that *Nil admirari,* the avoidance of troubles and dangers, and the retired life bring virtue.

Boscán, on the other hand, presents first the Neoplatonic idea of ascending spiritually to a vision of the Godhead, and then reports that the attainment of this height is what brings *Nil admirari,* virtue, and the "vida descansada." It is, in short, precisely the opposite of Mendoza's method; for "casto amor," with all its Neoplatonic implications, fosters the good life, and not vice versa. Boscán thus reverses the Stoic process of becoming a sage by implying that one must first become spiritually fit to participate in the classical ideals, whereas Mendoza implied that such a participation was what brought spiritual fitness. Mendoza, for example, tells Boscán, Marfira, and his friends that they should come to his classical world in the country if they wish to "vivir medianamente." Boscán, on the contrary, leaves the country to see his friends in the city, because once one has ascended to the spiritual state of Christian virtue it is no longer necessary to flee the dangers and illusions of civilization.

The same reversal is what allows Boscán to praise married life and even to accredit it with his achieving "la buena medianía." Because he rose from the dominance by the passions of crude love to the virtuous state of chaste love he can now enjoy the idyllic life of the classical authors. For this reason, Boscán states, one fourth of the way into his epistle, that in order to follow the golden mean he has married ("Y así por seguir aquesta vía, / heme casado con una muger"). He then describes the retired life in the first person plural, for it is profitable solely because the two are together. The description of their blissful marriage is unparalleled in traditional Spanish literature, where the female is either an adored object, a capricious and confusing impediment, or simply unmentioned.

In sum, Boscán's epistle follows closely the format and themes of Mendoza's letter; but Boscán made changes that altered radically the message of the poem. He stressed Christian themes, hetero-sexual love, a personal plan of life based on the equally classic gold-en mean rather than the ideal of Stoic perfection, an explicit appre-ciation for life in the city, and marriage as a peaceful compromise between the unattainable ideal of Stoic detachment and the Petrar-chan torments of youthful promiscuity.[12] As a necessary prerequis-ite to these alterations, Boscán fomented the Neoplatonic doctrine of ascending from this visible world of illusions to that invisible world of reality, whereby one automatically attains virtue. It is a program which, as A. A. Parker has demonstrated,[13] will permeate the Spanish literature of the Golden Age; and as A. G. Reichen-berger noted in his often cited study: "Guided by classical models Boscán tries to create something new out of the classical heritage, contemporary Italian Neo-Platonic ideology, and his own expe-rience and observations" ("Boscán's *Epístola a Mendoza,*" p. 17).

V *"Royal Octave"*

The last work in Book Three is also the most sophisticated. It is a one-thousand-and-eighty-line (one-hundred-thirty-five strophe) poem in hendecasyllabic royal octaves rhyming abababcc. The sub-ject matter is an amplification of a four-hundred line (fifty strophe) work by the Italian humanist Pietro Bembo (1470–1547) entitled "Stanze per festa carnascialesca, in lode di Amore" (1507).[14] Boscán's poem is charged with the same magnificent Renaissance spirit that is found in Bembo's, and with a very original sensitivity. It is humanist in its espousal of Neoplatonic themes, in its constant references to the classics, in its use of mythology, in its direct appeal for earthly love, and in its use of the elegant royal octave, which Boscán and Garcilaso de la Vega introduced into Spain. The spirit and tone of the poem, although in considerable part bor-rowed from Bembo, are totally new to Spanish letters. "Octava rima" begins thusly:

1.   En el lumbroso y fértil Oriente
       adonde más el cielo está templado,
       vive una sosegada y dulce gente,
       la qual en solo amor pone el cuidado.
       Esta jamás padece otro acidente
       sino es aquel que amores han causado;

aquí gobierna y siempre gobernó
aquella reina que en la mar nació.

2.   Aquí su cetro y su corona tiene,
     y desde aquí sus dádivas reparte;
     aquí su ley y su poder mantiene
     mucho mejor que en otra qualquier parte;
     aquí si querelloso alguno viene,
     sin quexa y sin pesar luego se parte;
     aquí se gozan todos en sus llamas,
     presentes las figuras de sus damas. (p. 424)

(In the bright and fertil East
where the heavens are more temperate,
lives a quiet and sweet people
who put their cares only in loving.
They never suffer any other accidents
but ones that love has caused;
here governs and always governed
that queen who in the sea was born.

Here she has her scepter and her crown,
and from here she reparts her boons;
here she maintains her law and her power
much better than in any other part;
here if some complaining soul comes,
without a complaint and without sorrow he then departs;
here all take pleasure in its flames,
with the figures of their ladies present.)

The first stanza is a copy of Bembo's initial strophe ("Ne l'odorato e lucido Oriente, / la sotto 'l puro e temperato cielo");[15] but the next thirty-two strophes are wholly original with Boscán, and the subsequent ones until stanza fifty-six are taken from various classical sources.

The first part of "Octava real" describes Amor's fabulous city, where love is the only topic of conversation, the only business, the only game; the edifices, rocks, fountains, rivers, winds, and fields represent and declare love. Love's house is there, on a green plain by a river with trees along its banks; the trees are full of flowers, and nightingales continually sing from the branches. This *locus amoenus* is surrounded by a thousand huts built of different kinds of wood, and in them the lovers meet to declare their demands and replies.

From this simple description it can be seen clearly that Boscán has entered totally into the Renaissance. The light tone, the new and rich vocabulary, the elegant royal octave, all are characteristic of the new cultural universe. The god of love is totally different also. The notion that Amor lives in a beautiful palace set in a pastoral scene characterized by harmony, serenity, joy, and verdure simply did not exist in Medieval times.[16]

Love, the poet continues in stanza eight, is armed with gold and lead arrows with which to impart desire or hate in the lovers. She mounts a tall tower and from there shoots anyone whom she desires. Amor also has a thousand cupids whose task is to instill the baser kinds of love, those that are satisfied in dark, dirty corners rather than in beds or drawing-rooms. Another person who also inhabits this kingdom is Jealousy. From her house come the thunder and the lightning. Love has many times attempted to close Jealousy's palace and free the people in it, but it is impossible; so Love sustains them and tries to correct them. Amor is constantly surrounded by all the conquered lovers, and she visits the residents of her town every day, spreading delight and gaiety.

One day Love decided to have a general meeting. Everyone came, and Love's son seated them in order according to the quality of their cares. She saw that some of the lovers were so fearful and sad that it was pathetic; so she decided to send reformers throughout the world to moderate the tormented souls. She ordered them to eliminate all those people who abuse or mock love, especially the women who tantalize their admirers only to reject them later. These women exist in all the world, but they especially abound in Spain.

Barcelona, which is the most beautiful city in the world and has the most charming ladies, also is the most disrespectful to love. Two particular damsels of that city, who because of their great beauty should be Love's companions, have become two Lucifers against her and are causing many other ladies to turn away from love also. So the goddess sends two special ambassadors and her son Cupid to convince the ladies that they should soften their hearts.

To this point (stanza 56: "Conviene para esto que os partáis"), Boscán has been working from his own imagination, following only very generally Bembo's plot. Now Boscán returns to imitate closely the Italian's "Stanze." Strophe fifty-six is a copy of Bembo's stanza eleven and the remainder is an expanded imitation of the source poem. This is especially true of stanzas fifty-six through eighty, which follow strophes eleven through twenty-two in "Stanze." Boscán usually expands his source, but in some cases he actually suppresses Bembo's verses, as with strophes 30–31, 33–34, 39, and 40 in the Italian version. According to Menéndez Pelayo (*Boscán,* p. 290), these stanzas were eliminated as material because of their erotic nature.

The tale continues as the two ambassadors set out for Spain, crossing the Nile, passing over Crete and Rhodes, Greece and Venice, Italy and France, until they reach Barcelona. Early the next day, they seek out the two ladies and speak to first one and then the other. The remainder of the poem (seventy-two stanzas) is the argument by the ambassadors to convince the women that they should respond to amour's call. It is similar in many ways to Garcilaso's "Oda a la flor de Knido," even to the extent of using the tale of Anaxarate as the example of what happens to ladies to reject honest love. The ambassadors begin by asking what error has led the two damsels to declare war against love, since love has given birth to every living thing (the section is inspired by Bembo's strophe 17):

> 68.   Amor es voluntad dulce y sabrosa,
> que todo corazón duro enternece;
> el amor es el alma en toda cosa,
> por quien remoza el mundo y reverdece;
> el fin de todos en amor reposa,
> en él todo comienza y permanece,
> deste mundo y del otro la gran traza:
> con sus brazos amor todo la abraza. (p. 443)

> (Love is a sweet and delightful will,
> that makes every hard heart tender;
> love is the soul of all things
> for which the world rejuvenates and renews life;
> the end of everything rests in love,
> in it all begins and remains,
> the great artifice of this world and the next:
> with its arms love embraces it all.)

Without it, the ambassadors continue, there would be no pleasure or glory, nothing to raise human thoughts, nothing to enrich the memory and the understanding. Love lifts us to great heights and sustains us there; love governs all created things and gives order to creation: earth, sea, air, fire, the visible as well as the invisible, the mutable as well as the eternal. Love even moves the stars and sends virtue to every part of the universe; it raises our corporeal bodies to great heights, allowing us to breathe the air of the heavens. Love moved the pens of Ovid, Tibullus, Propertius, Petrarch, Cino de Pistoia, Juan de Mena, Francisco de la Torre, Garci-Sánchez de Badajoz, Luis de Haro, and Garcilaso de la Vega. Love caused the two ladies to be born, and so it is extremely unjust for them not to recognize its power; for their not loving causes them to reside in the darkest night, where they will never bear fruit nor flowers. If these arguments do not convince them, perhaps examples from ancient fables will, especially those in which disdainful women were turned into hard stone.

Finally, the ambassadors point out how creatures without love have no purpose in the world, and how the tree that does not bear fruit is cut down. Yet those things that promise a harvest, like the grain, are tenderly cared for by the laborers. If only the two ladies would accept love, they would see how better life could be. They would sleep peacefully at night, they would be content all day; and, of most importance, they would be following their natural inclinations:

> 110.   El eternal y universal maestro
>   quando las cosas fabricó y compuso,
>   en todas, por el bien y placer nuestro,
>   un principio de fuego de amor puso;
>   por esta razón, pues, que agora os muestro,
>   lo natural también vuestro os dispuso
>   a tener de aquel fuego la simiente,
>   que está en el corazón naturalmente.   (p. 455)

> (The eternal and universal master
> when he composed and fabricated all things,
> in all, for our good and our pleasure,
> put the principle of love's fire;
> for this reason, then, I now show you
> that he disposed you also to what is natural

to have the seed of that fire
that is naturally in the heart.)

And they have it, the ambassadors explain, but it is almost extin-
guished by harshness and unnatural habits. It is like a flint, and if
they would just let it be struck by desire, the fire would consume
the whole world. They should therefore love as is proper for them
to do; and if they do, they will also bring joy to their respective
courtiers. Employing the *Collige rosas* topos, the envoys advise the
women to respond to love's promptings; for, if they resist, it may
soon be too late:

132.   Guardá que mientras el buen tiempo dura,
         no se os pierda la fresca primavera;
         salí a gozar el campo y su verdura,
         antes que todo en el invierno muera.   (p. 461)

         (Be careful that while the good weather lasts,
         you do not lose the fresh Spring;
         go out to take pleasure in the field and its greenness,
         before all dies in the Winter.)

These arguments should surely convince the ladies of their error, so
the ambassadors end their discourse and declare they will return the
next day for the reply. The poem thus ends without the reader
knowing whether the two damsels decide to accept or reject love.
Cardinal Bembo's poem ends the same way, so one must assume
that Boscán never intended to write the reply to the envoys.

Juan Boscán has come a long way from the passion and torment
of the courtly lover who lives solely to serve his lady in hopes of
some small sign of favor. He has entered the world of pagan
humanism, where the direct appeal to earthly love is couched in
purely hedonistic terms. The style is totally different also, for
Boscán has a new feeling for the beauties of the natural world —
the descriptions of the countryside around Amor's city are
Boscán's own — and he has adjusted to the gentler and more flowing rhythm of the Italianate hendecasyllable. He has become, in
short, a true Renaissance man, who can say with the other humanists: *Homo sum, humani nihil a me alienum puto.*

CHAPTER 5

Conclusions

OVER four hundred years after his death, Juan Boscán's renown continues to depend principally on his role as the introducer of Italian meters into Spain. Indeed, it was he or his friend Garcilaso de la Vega who first published Spanish verses in *terza rima, canzone, sonetto, verso sciolto,* and *ottava rima,* all of which employ the Petrarchan hendecasyllable. Garcilaso, moreover, initiated on his own the Italian *lira* and the *rima al mezzo.* Boscán and Garcilaso were also the first Spaniards to utilize these rhyme schemes in the Renaissance *storia* or light epic, the Horatian epistle, the Italian *epistola,* the *capitolo,* and the festive poetic form known simply as *stanze.* For solely these accomplishments Juan Boscán deserves the acclaim rendered him as the father of Renaissance poetry in Spain, the innovator of Spanish meters in the sixteenth century, and the head of the Italianate school.

Perhaps of more importance, Juan Boscán, along with his collaborator Garcilaso de la Vega, was the initiator of the Renaissance spirit in Spain. He was born, in fact, at the dawn of the Spanish Renaissance in 1492, when Columbus discovered America, when the Catholic Monarchs took the last Arab stronghold in Granada, when the Jews were ousted from the peninsula, and when Antonio de Nebrija published the first modern grammar for a vernacular language. He was educated at the court of King Ferdinand V, the first enlightened European monarch; and he served under Charles I, the first European empire builder. He came into direct contact with every knowledgeable personage of his time, and was evidently known, admired, and respected by them all. Juan Boscán, in short, was born at precisely the right time, knew precisely the right people, and was given precisely the right opportunity to inscribe his name into Spanish literary history. He took advantage of each and

every propitious moment, and he did it with the grace of a true
Renaissance courtier. Juan Boscán was not born a Renaissance man. His poetry in
Book One testifies to that. He was born into an intellectual ambience totally medieval, yet he somehow managed to shift in the
prime of his life to a new realm of thought and sensibility. Few
poets of any other epoch have managed to change so completely
their *Weltanschauung* as did Juan Boscán. All those other medieval
poets and thinkers, all the traditionalists, remained medieval and
traditionalist until they died. None of the new Renaissance men
bothered to investigate the preceding cosmos they considered so
alien to their new ways of thought. No Aristotelians became Platonists, no songbook writers became sonneteers, no courtly lovers
married and wrote poetry about it. The only other example in
Spanish history of an equivalent changing of directions is the
painter Francisco José de Goya y Lucientes (1746-1828). Like Boscán, Goya began to paint in the "old" style, and he was perhaps
the best artist in that medium, as Boscán was undoubtedly considered to be the best courtly poet of his time. With the advent of
Romanticism and the rejection of the optimistic social and aesthetic
values of good taste, however, Goya took the great leap, as did
Boscán, into the next cultural age to become the initiator of the
"new" way of painting. The transference was so totally complete
that the paintings of the two periods seem to have been done by two
different people, and in a sense they were. The same is true for
Boscán's poetry.

   The chronological trajectory of Boscán's artistic metamorphosis
is explicitly delineated in the organization that the poet imposed on
his works. Book One contains the Castilian lyrics that he wrote
under the influence of the pervasive *cancionero* tradition of Spanish poetry. Although there is no absolute proof, it is convenient to
presume that those endeavors were undertaken before 1526, the
year the Spaniard was urged by Andrea Navaggiero to experiment
with the Italian meters. All the poems in Book One are composed in
arte menor and utilize the traditional forms termed *coplas, canciones,* and *villancicos.* The tone, style, structure, and language par-
take of the medieval courtly love poesy that flourished throughout
the fifteenth century in Spain and reached its culmination in the
1511 *Cancionero general* compiled by Hernando del Castillo.
Boscán's lyrics, in fact, are in no way different from those of his

predecessors. The entire corpus of the *cancionero* poetry is so uniformly homogeneous that if Boscán's name were not on his works there would be no way of telling who the author was.

As did his contemporaries, Boscán viewed love in Aristotelian terms as a psychosomatic infirmity that seizes the lover and afflicts him with intense physical pain and mental anguish. It was thus properly denominated "mal amor," "crudo amor," and even "loco amor." The only saving grace for courtly love was its cathartic ability; the burning passion experienced by the lover supposedly cremated all the baser elements in his system, thereby purifying his sensibilities and imbuing his soul with the *fin' amors* necessary for proper service. The lover, through interminable suffering and torment, thus eventually becomes acceptable by his lady for recognition because of the purified state his passion achieves. Along with his physical purgation of gross matter, there is a highly orchestrated courtly love regimen to which the troubadour must adhere. It includes service, courtesy, secrecy, humility, self-imposed absence, the acceptance of obstacles, and total chastity. Boscán describes and follows all of these tenets in his Castilian lyrics with nothing new, innovative, or exceptional to offer.

The 1544 edition of Book One terminates with a long poem entitled "Boscán's Conversion" (see Appendix C). It is a perfect courtly palinode, rejecting the pain and suffering, the endless years of service and longing, the wasted tears and constant fear, for a return to "lo divinal." The poem is a sine qua non for all Medieval bards who outlive the amorous fancy. Courtly love is a cul-de-sac that prohibits access to the normal avenues of social life, such as marriage and propagation, and it is also contrary in its sublimation of the flesh and its descending adoration of Eros to the dictates of Christian fellowship and charity. The normal person thus eventually has to abandon the game or succumb to a sterile existence in the jailhouse of love. Boscán chooses the former option.

Book Two of Boscán's poetry is prefaced by his famous letter to the Duchess of Somma (see Appendix A) in which he declares that his poetry in Italian meters is new for Spain and better than anything that has come before. Book Two contains all the sonnets and Italianate *canciones* written by Boscán, and they are in the sequence that the poet chose for them. They describe what Boscán calls "la historia de mis males," and they demonstrate beautifully the radical transformation in thought that the poet achieved.

The first seventy-six sonnets prove indisputably the Spaniard's mastery of the Italian rhyme scheme and meter. The poems are true sonnets, differing in no way from the thousands of others that will be written by his successors; yet their tone is wholly courtly. Boscán had attained command of the techniques necessary to write the new poetry, but he had yet to master the Renaissance spirit of the Italian poets. The hendecasyllable and its appropriate forms — sonnet, *terza rima, canción,* royal octave, and blank verse — did not therefore contain within their structure the refined sensibility, harmonious and symmetrical syntax, or chaste love that separate the medieval mind from the Renaissance joy of life. That had to be learned apart; but when it was, the structure was there to receive it. Form, in this case, came long before content.

The integration of the new sensibility with the new structures appears in Sonnet Seventy-Seven, and remains dominant in all the remaining sonnets. There is no evidence to explain why or how Boscán suddenly changed his spiritual attitudes the way he did. It is convenient to assume, nevertheless, his translating of *Il cortegiano* in 1533 to be the turning point; for in that masterpiece by Baldassare Castiglione are found all the ingredients necessary to fabricate the new *Weltanschauung.* All the parts of Boscán's poems, both content and form as well as overall effect, now work together to present a comprehensive picture of poetic sensibility. The tone is clearly Platonic rather than Aristotelian. Love is an act of the rational faculties, a spiritual orexis that nullifies the desires of the appetites. As opposed to the cathartic sublimation of the flesh to reach *fin' amors,* the Renaissance Platonist uses his reason to move from the visible to the invisible, from the physical to the spiritual. It is a process of depuration achieved by methodically stripping away one layer of gross matter after another, as if reality were an onion, until the pure idealic form beneath the matter is revealed. Michelangelo Buonarroti's sculptures, especially the unfinished ones, are the examples par excellence of this procedure. Boscán's technique cannot be so clearly delineated but he participated in the same aesthetic.

Canción Ten and Sonnet Ninety are the last two poems in Book Two. They describe spiritual changes that Boscán underwent when he rejected the antiquated Aristotelian philosophy of life. The *canción* is closer to "Boscán's Conversion" than to Sonnet Ninety because it expresses a totally religious conversion rather than a movement of the soul to a more spiritual kind of love. The sonnet expressly embraces "el casto amor," a new sensibility characterized by a gentle fire in the soul rather than by a raging inferno. It functions in relation to the new spirit of the later sonnets in the same way that "Boscán's Conversion" and *Canción* Ten functioned for the courtly love described in the *coplas,* early sonnets and Italianate *canciones.*

The third part of Boscán's poetic corpus contains all the later pieces (i.e., after 1526) that are not sonnets or Italianate *canciones.* The only love poetry, interestingly, is of the earlier mental framework. "Chapter I" and "Epistle" are both courtly in nature, describing Boscán's desire to serve his lady, although the former exhibits clear influences from the Neoplatonic school in its description of the beloved as an embodiment of all that is good capable of inducing his understanding to ascend to the realm of ideas. "Epístola" was definitely written before the early 1530s, and "Capítulo I" was probably composed before the other pieces in Book Three but after the poems in the first two books.

"Leander and Hero" and "Royal Octave" have love as their central theme also, but they do not describe Boscán's love. They thus express a significant objectivity on the bard's part, for he has now reached the poetic maturity to utilize his artistry in a non-egocentric way, something that was sorely difficult for any of the medieval poets to do. The two poems also show the greater objectivity of their author in their clear narrative style and blatant avoidance of Christian elements. Neither, moreover, is "Spanish"; the story of Leander and Hero takes place in Turkey, and the "Royal Octave" begins in the East and ends with a *Collige rosas* discourse delivered to two disdainful women who only by happenstance reside in Barcelona. Both pieces are consummate Renaissance works of art. There is not one thing medieval about either one of them; so they testify without the shadow of a doubt to the thorough elimination of one way of thought and the complete espousal of another that Boscán somehow executed.

The most indicative work in Book Three is the "Epistle to Mendoza." It stands in relation to its section as Sonnet Ninety did to Book Two and "Boscán's Conversion" did to Book One. The basic themes — *Nil admirari, Virtus, Aurea mediocritas, Beatus ille* — are all culled from Diego Hurtado de Mendoza's epistle to Boscán, but the Catalan's sweeping acceptance and sincere espousal of them show how deeply imbued his character was with the humanist philosophy. Boscán also elaborated other material unmentioned by Mendoza, such as the Platonic ascent to spiritual maturity, the idyllic promise of married life, the avocation of moderation in following the golden mean, and the rational compromise between city life and country life. All of these things point to a well-rounded, mature person who is totally at peace with himself and his environment, something that certainly could not be said about the author of the poems in Book One.

In sum, Juan Boscán has become what is called a "Renaissance man," a person embodying broad intellectual and cultural interests who guides his life according to the classical ideals of virtue, common sense, self-knowledge, control of the appetites, and right reason. In this, Boscán even surpasses his friend and collaborator Garcilaso de la Vega.

The final concern regards Juan Boscán's merit as a poet. He is not as adept at defining emotional sensibilities as are Garcilaso de la Vega, Luis de León, San Juan de la Cruz, Luis de Góngora, and Francisco de Quevedo; yet he is head and shoulders above any of his contemporaries. His *coplas* are clearly of a higher quality than the poems in the *Cancionero general*. His sonnets and *canciones* are, with the exception of Garcilaso's, the best available until the entrance of Fernando de Herrera; and to find anything that matches the brilliance of the "Epistle to Mendoza" one has to await the publication of the "Epístola moral a Fabio." "Leander and Hero" remains the finest and most humanistic Renaissance light epic for years to come, and "Royal Octave" is the unrivalled paragon of the Renaissance sense of gaiety and joy of life. So Juan Boscán may not be the best Spanish bard, nor even the best Renaissance poet; but he is certainly equal to anyone else writing poetry during his lifetime.

Notes and References

Chapter One

1. Biographical data are taken from Martín de Riquer, *Juan Boscán y su cancionero barcelonés* (Barcelona: Archivo Histórico — Casa del Arcediano, 1945).

2. This date is cited by Arnold G. Reichenberger, "Boscán and the Classics," *Classical Literature,* III (1951), 97.

3. For a comprehensive biography of Marineo (Marinis), see Caro Lynn, *A College Professor of the Renaissance: Lucio Marineo Sículo among the Spanish Humanists* (Chicago: University of Chicago Press, 1937).

4. The two traditional studies on Hispano-Italian relations during the Renaissance are Felipe Picatoste, *Estudios sobre la grandeza y decadencia de España* (Madrid: Imprenta de la viuda de Hernando, 1887), 3 vols. (Vol. I, "España e Italia"; Vol. II, "El ejercito español en Italia"); and Benedetto Croce, *La Spagna nella vita italiana durante la Rinascenza* (Bari: G. Laterza, 1917), translated into Spanish as *España en la vida italiana del Renacimiento* (Buenos Aires: Ediciones Imán, 1945).

5. For a biography of Navaggiero, see Antonio María Fabié, ed., *Viajes por España* (Madrid: F. Fé, 1879), pp. xc-cliii.

6. *La trajectoria poética de Garcilaso* (Madrid: Gredos, 1968), pp. 23–24: "El amor es concebido como un culto y un servicio; este vasallaje espiritual dignifica al enamorado, apartándole de pensamientos viles e infundiendo en él ansias de superación. La poesía explora, más o menos escolásticamente, las galerías del alma, subrayando los contrastes entre la razón y el deseo, entre la visión objetiva del mundo y el enfoque personal del individuo. Hijas de la lucha interior y del comportamiento esquivo de la amada son la tristeza y la inestabilidad de ánimo. Los enamorados se entregan a su dolor, gozan saboreando el sufrimiento y paladean con fruición las lágrimas vertidas. Sin embargo, este placer del *martire* no impide que cuenten pesarosos los años de servidumbre."

7. Good discussions in English of March's poetry can be found in Gerald Brenan, *The Literature of the Spanish People* (New York: Meridian Books, 1957), pp. 108–14; and in Arthur Terry, *Catalan Literature* (London and New York: Barnes & Noble, 1972), pp. 39–75.

8. "Poesía de cancionero y poesía italianizante," *De la edad media a nuestros días* (Madrid: Gredos, 1967), pp. 152–53: "El moroso discurrir de endecasílabos y heptasílabos repudiaba la expresión directa y el realismo pintoresco frecuentes en los cancioneros; en cambio, era el ritmo adecuado para la exploración del propio yo en detenidos análisis, y para expresar el arrobo contemplativo ante la naturaleza. Estos eran los dos grandes temas de la nueva escuela. Petrarca había dado la pauta para el escrutinio de los estados de alma. Los poetas, al explorar el propio espíritu, cobraban conciencia de sí mismos y contribuían así al descubrimiento del individuo, el hecho capital del Renacimiento."

9. See Marcelino Menéndez Pelayo, *Antología de poetas líricos castellanos: Boscán,* in *Obras completas* (Santander: CSIC, 1945), XXVI, 148. Much of what follows on the hendecasyllable comes from Chapter XLIII of this anthology and from Pedro Henríquez Ureña, "El endecasílabo castellano," *Estudios de versificación española* (Buenos Aires: Universidad de Buenos Aires, 1961), pp. 271–347.

10. It is interesting to note that Boscán and all the other poets and scholars after him believed Ausias March to be a precursor or at least a contemporary of Dante Alighiere. Many, because of this anachronism, believed Petrarch actually imitated the poetry of Ausias March (See Menéndez Pelayo, p. 147).

11. Years later the same tactic is going to be used against the poets of the Gongoran school, who will be called *culteranos* (from *luteranos*).

12. "El mismo hizo a nuestra poesía no dever nada en la diversidad i magestad de la compostura a la Italiana, siendo en la delicadeza de los conceptos igual con ella, i no inferior en darlos a entender i espressarlos, como alguno de los mismos italianos confiessa." Cited by Elias L. Rivers, "Garcilaso divorciado de Boscán," in *Homenaje a Rodríguez Moñino* (Madrid: Castalia, 1966), II, 121.

13. "Mas como quiera que sea, todos los que impresos por imprimir en aquel exemplar se hallaron yo los traduxe en coplas a la italiana (que eso quise decir quando las llamé rhimas, que ansí llaman ellos sus coplas) porque vía que vosotros os davades ya más a ellas como a más artificiosas, y ansí mesmo eran más al propósito porque en pocos versos se dize más que en las otras castellanas que ya todos llamáys redondillas" ("Prefación de Bernardino Daza Pinciano sobre los Emblemas de Alciato traducidos por él mismo, a sus amigos," *Los emblemas de Alciato traducidos en rhimas españolas* [Lyons: Mathias Bonhomme, 1549], p. 13).

14. *The Book of the Courtier,* trans. Charles S. Singleton (Garden City: Anchor Books, 1959), p. 43.

15. Castiglione's life has been described in detail by Julia Cartwright Ady, *The Perfect Courtier: Baldassare Castiglione, His Life and Letters, 1478-1529* (New York: E.P. Dutton, 1927), 2 vols.

16. For full bibliographical references, see José Simón Díaz, *Bibliografía de la literatura hispánica*, VI (Madrid: CSIC, 1973), 622-34.

17. The term is from Gian Roberto Sorolla, "Boscán as Translator: St. Jerome or the Humanists?", *Modern Language Notes,* LXXVII (1962), 187-91. Sorolla explains that there were three normal ways to translate in the Renaissance: *conversio ad verbum* (a pedantically literal translation), *transferre ad sententiam* (a faithful oratorical translation), and *immutare* (a free oratorical translation). Boscán used the last method, as can be seen from his use of "mudar" as opposed to "romanzar."

18. As early as 1536 the Portuguese writer Sa de Miranda refers to the Italianate poetry of Boscán and Garcilaso as if he knew it quite well (see Menéndez Pelayo, p. 338).

19. The first edition has been reproduced in facsimile twice this century: Salamanca, 1936; and Madrid, 1943. For a full bibliographical account of all other printings, see the bibliography of Simón Díaz.

20. For complete details, see Rivers, pp. 121-29.

Chapter Two

1. See the comments of Luis Alfonso de Carballo, *Cisne de Apolo* (1602), ed. Alberto Porqueras Mayo (Madrid: CSIC, 1958), I, 220-28.

2. See J. B. Trend, "Musical Settings of Famous Poets," *Revue Hispanique,* LXXI (1927), 547.

3. A study of courtly love in Spain in all its aspects, including sight, is in Otis H. Green, *Spain and the Western Tradition* (Madison: University of Wisconsin Press, 1968), I, 72-300.

4. Consult M. Menéndez Pelayo, *Boscán,* pp. 209-69; and Rafael Lapesa, *Trayectoria,* pp. 19-53.

5. R. Lapesa, in "Poesía de cancionero," p. 148, affirms that the only sure influence of Petrarch on Spanish poetry before Boscán is in the lyrics of the Marqués de Santillana.

6. Carballo comments: "Copla es un ayu[n]tamie[n]to y copula de cierto numero de versos subjeta a cierta orden de consonancias. Y ansi se llama copla de este verbo copulo por ayuntar" (*Cisne de Apolo,* I, 196).

7. For a detailed description of Petrarch's sequence, consult Germaine Warkentin, "'Love's Sweetest Part, Variety:' Petrarch and the Curious Frame of the Renaissance Sonnet Sequence," *Renaissance and Reformation,* XI (1973), 14-23.

8. "Notes on the Chronology of Boscán's Verses," *Modern Philology,* XXV (1927-28), 29-36.

9. *Las treinta de Juan Boscán,* ed. Hayward Keniston (New York: Hispanic Society of America, 1911).

10. This form of the *copla real* is described in Tomás Navarro, *Métrica española* (Syracuse: Syracuse University Press, 1956), pp. 111-12.

124 JUAN BOSCÁN

11. The palinode as a necessity in the courtly literary tradition is discussed in *Spanish Poetry of the Golden Age,* ed., Bruce W. Wardropper (New York: Appleton-Century-Crofts, 1971), pp. 47–61.

12. For a full discussion, see Robert Edward Brennan, *Thomistic Psychology* (New York: Macmillan, 1941). A more general explanation is given by Herschel Baker, *The Image of Man* (New York: Harper Torchbooks, 1961), Chapter XVII. The most famous treatise on faculty psychology in Spain is the *Tratado del alma* by Juan Luis Vives (1492–1540).

13. Vives explains: "Creado el hombre para la felicidad eterna, se le ha concedido la facultad de aspirar al bien, para que desee unirse a él. Esta facultad se llama voluntad. Y como no se puede desear lo que no se conoce, existe a este fin otra facultad, que se llama inteligencia. Además, nuestro espíritu no permanece siempre en un mismo pensamiento, sino que pasa de unos a otros, por lo cual necesita un cierto depósito en que, al presentarse los nuevos, conserve los anteriores como tesoro de cosas ahora ausentes, las cuales reproduzca y tome cuando es menester. El nombre de esta función es la memoria" (*Tratado del alma* [Madrid: Espasa-Calpe, 1942], p. 54).

14. See Tomás Navarro, pp. 107–10.

15. It was first published by Martín de Riquer in *Juan Boscán y su cancionero barcelonés* (Barcelona: Archivo Histórico — Casa del Arcediano, 1945).

Chapter Three

1. "No sólo fue innovador en la forma métrica, sino en la forma íntima y substancial de la poesía. En sus sonetos y en sus canciones el amor está tomado por lo serio, y aunque todavía nos parezca metafísico y vago, tiene de vez en cuando accentos de sinceridad que no engañan. Sólo escribiendo en endecasílabos llega Boscán a cierto grado de emoción poética, entreverada alguna vez con graciosos detalles realistas. Nada o casi nada de esto hay en sus versos cortos, aunque sean más correctos de lengua y de ritmo" (*Boscán,* p. 210).

2. See J. G. Fucilla, "Notes on Spanish Renaissance Poetry," *Philological Quarterly,* XI (1932), 225–62.

3. The sonnet is number XXXV in Petrarch's *Il canzionere,* ed. Dino Provenzal (Milan, 1954). All references to Petrarch's verse will be to the poem number in this edition. For a comprehensive study of the influence of both Petrarch's and Ausias March's poetry on Juan Boscán's sonnets, consult Thaddeus C. Porter, "The Italianate Poetry of Juan Boscán," Diss. Vanderbilt 1968, pp. 61–114.

4. Most recently, the sonnet has been included in Arthur Terry, *An Anthology of Spanish Poetry, Part I: 1500–1580* (Oxford: Pergamon Press, 1965), p. 38; Elias L. Rivers, *Renaissance and Baroque Poetry of*

Spain (New York: Dell Publishing Co., 1966), pp. 31–32; and Bruce W. Wardropper, *Spanish Poetry of the Golden Age* (New York: Appleton-Century-Crofts, 1971), pp. 228–29.

5. See the exhaustive study of Leo Spitzer, "Classical and Christian Ideas of World Harmony," *Traditio,* II (1944), 409–64 and III (1945), 307–64.

6. Leon Hebreo, *Diálogos de amor,* trans. Inca Garcilaso de la Vega (Buenos Aires: Espasa-Calpe, 1947), p. 16: "Y así como hay tres suertes de bueno: provechoso, deleitable y honesto, así hay tres suertes de amor. El uno es el deleitable, el otro es el provechoso, y el otro el honesto." For the elaboration of these categories in the pastoral novel, consult my study "Renaissance Platonism and the Spanish Pastoral Novel," *Hispania,* LII (1969), 387–88.

7. Sonnet LXXXIV is cited and commented upon as typically Platonic by María Pilar Aparici Llanos in her study "Teorías amorosas en la lírica castellana del Siglo XVI," *Boletín de la Biblioteca de Menéndez Pelayo,* XLIV (1968), 121–67.

8. "Creo que la diferencia entre un amor y otro está en el hecho de que para el platónico el amor es una virtud del entendimiento y el único camino para llegar al conocimiento de las ideas y por tanto hasta el Sumo Bien, mientras que la novela sentimental, fruto tardío de la cultura gótica, está basada sobre el concepto escolástico del amor, pasión del apetito concupiscible que, aunque puede ser resistida por el albedrío o moderada por la voluntad, frecuentemente la domina, oscureciendo el entendimiento, hasta el punto de que dipute lo malo por bueno. Tal desorden de nuestras potencias es lo que les da a las novelas sentimentales ese aire tormentoso y aborrascado que tanto contrasta con la serena melancolía de las pastorales, donde hasta las lágrimas son melodiosas y están sometidas a ritmo y compás, como el verso y como la música. Es decir, que si para los unos el amor es virtud cognoscitiva, para los otros es enfermedad del alma, que en muchos casos lleva a la muerte." Cited from the introduction to Jorge de Montemayor, *Los siete libros de la Diana* (Madrid: Editora Nacional, 1976), pp. xiv–xv.

9. See Rafael Lapesa, *Introducción a los estudios literarios* (Salamanca: Anaya, 1971), pp. 98–99.

10. *La canción petrarquista en la lírica española del siglo de oro* (Madrid: CSIC, 1949), pp. 247–49.

11. Op. cit., p. 48.

12. See E. Allison Peers, "The Alleged Debts of San Juan de la Cruz to Boscán and Garcilaso de la Vega," *Hispanic Review,* XXI (1953), 1–19 and 93–106.

Chapter Four

1. "Boscán and the Classics," *Comparative Literature*, III (1951), 103.
2. For a complete explanation, consult Arnold G. Reichenberger, "Boscán and Ovid," *Modern Language Notes*, LXV (1950), 379–83.
3. "Boscán and *Il cortegiano:* The *Historia de Leandro y Hero*," *The Literary Mind of Medieval and Renaissance Spain* (Lexington: The University Press of Kentucky, 1970), p. 133.
4. *The Book of the Courtier*, trans. C. S. Singleton (Garden City: Anchor Books, 1959), p. 354.
5. Sources for this quaint anecdote about the Greek painter Timanthus (fl. 400 B.C.) are varied. Boscán could have culled it from Quintillian (*Institutio*, II, 13), from Pliny's *Natural History* (XXXV, 26.12), or from Chapter XXII of Cicero's *Brutus*. The use of the Iphigenia theme here gives substance to a hypothesis that the Greek play by Euripedes which Boscán supposedly translated was *Iphegenia in Aulis*.
6. For Horace's influence on Spanish letters, see M. Menéndez Pelayo, *Horacio en España* (Madrid, 1885), and María Rosa Lida de Malkiel, *La tradición clásica en España* (Barcelona: Editorial Ariel, 1975), pp. 253–67.
7. "The Horatian Epistle and its Introduction into Spanish Literature," *Hispanic Review*, XXII (1954), 186. Most of the historical data that follows comes from this splendid study.
8. *The Satires and Epistles of Horace* (Chicago and London: University of Chicago Press, 1959), p. 157.
9. For a complete account of Mendoza's life, read Erika Spivakovsky, *Son of the Alhambra: Don Diego Hurtado de Mendoza* (Austin and London: University of Texas Press, 1970).
10. *Moral Essays*, trans. John W. Basore (Cambridge and London: Loeb Classical Library, 1935): "Summum bonum est animus fortuita despiciens, virtute laetus" (p. 108); "Invicta vis animi, perita rerum, placida in actu cum humanitate multa et converdantium cura" (p. 108); "Potest beatus dici qui nece cupit nec timet beneficio rationis" (p. 110).
11. "Boscán's *Epístola a Mendoza*," *Hispanic Review*, XVII (1949), 17.
12. These particular innovations are culled from Rivers, "Horatian Epistle," pp. 191–93.
13. "Expansion and Scholarship in Spain," *The Age of the Renaissance*, ed. Denys Hay (London: McGraw-Hill, 1967), pp. 221–48.
14. For studies of Boscán's indebtedness to Bembo, see M. Menéndez Pelayo, *Boscán*, pp. 278–92; and T. C. Porter, pp. 191–96. This is the same Cardinal Bembo who gave the famous discourse on love in Castiglione's *Il cortegiano*.

15. *Opere in volgare,* ed. Mario Marti (Florence: Sansoni, 1961), p. 543.

16. This point has been firmly established by Francisco López Estrada, *Los libros de pastores en la literatura española: La órbita previa* (Madrid: Gredos, 1974).

Selected Bibliography

Juan Boscán's Works

Las obras de Boscán y algunas de Garcilasso de la Vega repartidas en quatro libros. Barcelona: Garles Amorós, 1543. This work, with slight additions and alterations, saw twenty-six printings in the sixteenth century and one printing in the seventeenth century. One twentieth century edition was done by F.S.R. (Madrid: Aguilar, 1944).

Las obras de Juan Boscán repartidas en tres libros. Ed. William I. Knapp. Madrid: Librería de M. Murillo, 1875. The first edition of Boscán's poetry separated from Garcilaso's. It contains the complete published works plus a number of *coplas* and *canciones* extant only in manuscripts. All citations in this Twayne volume are to Knapp's edition.

Obras poéticas. Ed. Martín de Riquer, Antonio Coma y Joaquín Molas. Barcelona: Facultad de Filosofía y Letras, 1957. The most complete edition of Boscán's poetic corpus.

Los quatro del cortesano compuestos en italiano por el conde Balthasar Castellón y agora nuevamente traduzidos en lengua castellana por Boscán. Barcelona: Pedro Monpezar, 1534. This translation of Baldassare Castiglione's *Il cortegiano* was reprinted fifteen times in the sixteenth century. The first modern critical edition was done by Antonio María Fabié (Madrid: Librería de los Bibliófilos, 1873). A number of printings have appeared in the twentieth century; the most notable ones are by Augusto F. Avilés (Madrid: CIAP, 1931; 2 vols.) and by the *Revista de Filología Española*, Anejo XXV (Madrid: CSIC, 1942), which has a preliminary study by M. Menéndez Pelayo.

Las treinta de Juan Boscán. Ed. Hayward Keniston. New York: The Hispanic Society of America, 1911. An edition of a *suelta* entitled *Coplas de Boscán nuevamente hechas,* printed in the second or third decade of the sixteenth century. The *copla* is "A tanto disimular" (XV).

Juan Boscán y su cancionero barcelonés. Transcripción, estudio y publicación de cien documentos desconocidos. Ed. Martín de Riquer. Barcelona: Ayuntamiento, 1945. One hundred documents pertaining to Juan Boscán and his family along with the facsimile of a manuscript containing nineteen poems by Boscán.

Coplas, sonetos y otras poesías. Ed. Manuel de Montoliu. Barcelona: Montaner y Simón, 1946. A collection of Boscán's best poetry. The introduction (pp. ix-xxxix) is an important contribution to Boscán scholarship.

SECONDARY SOURCES

Works on Juan Boscán

BONI, MARCO. "Nuove osservazioni intorno al petrarchismo di Juan Boscán." *Convivium,* X (1940), 78-85.

BUNTING, KENNETH E. *The poetry of Juan Boscán.* Diss. The University of North Carolina, 1967. A standard survey of Boscán's poetry that adds little to existing scholarship and criticism.

CRAWFORD, J. P. W. "Notes on Three Sonnets of Boscán." *Modern Language Notes,* XLI (1926), 102-5. Finds sources in Petrarch's poetry for the following sonnets by Boscán: "Dexadme en paz, o duros pensamientos" (XIII), "Bueno es amar? pues, cómo daña tanto?" (LV), and "Si un corazón de un verdadero amante" (LVII).

————. "Notes on the Chronology of Boscán's verses." *Modern Philology,* XXV (1927), 29-36. Postulates that Boscán's *coplas,* sonnets, and *canciones* each delineate the love life of the poet. *Coplas* I-XII describe a courtly affair frought with suffering, but *Coplas* XIII-XXV record a pure love on a higher plane. The course of this new love is described also in Sonnets XXVIII-XC. The *canciones* exhibit the same change.

DIEZ ECHARRI, E. "Boscán, el poeta innovador." *Arbor,* IV (1945), 32-47. An apology for Boscán, especially for his use of the hendecasyllable, against the harsh criticism of M. Menéndez Pelayo.

FLAMINI, FRANCISCO. "La 'Historia de Leandro y Hero' e l'ottava rima di Boscán." *Studi di storia letteraria italiana e straniera.* Livorno: Tip. di R. Guisti, 1895. Pp. 385-417.

FUCILLA, J. G. "Notes on Spanish Renaissance Poetry." *Philological Quarterly,* XI (1932), 225-62. Boscán has nineteen sonnets in which the tercets rhyme cde-cde, twenty-five in which they rhyme cdc-cdc, twenty-seven that rhyme cdc-dcd, twenty that rhyme cde-dce, and one (LXXVII) with tercets that rhyme cde-dec.

GREEN, OTIS H. "Boscán and *Il cortegiano:* The *Historia de Leandro y Hero.*" *Thesaurus,* IV (1948), 90-101. Republished in *The Literary Mind of Medieval & Renaissance Spain* (Lexington: The University Press of Kentucky, 1970), pp. 133-40. Shows how Boscán, under the influence of Castiglione, reshaped Musaeus' pagan lover into a Neoplatonic courtier.

_____. "On *Natura* in Boscán." *Hispanic Review,* XVII (1949), 71-73. Refutes a statement of Manuel de Montoliu that Boscán's idea of nature as a creative force (*Natura naturans*) was new for the time. Green shows that the notion pervades medieval thought.

HOMENAJE *a Boscán en el IV centenario de su muerte (1542-1942).* Barcelona: Biblioteca Central, 1944. Catalog of a bibliographical exhibition and the text of a speech given by Ramón Peres.

HORNEDO, RAFAEL MARIA DE. "Boscán y la célebre estrofa XI del *Cántico espiritual.*" *Razón y fe,* CXXVIII (1943), 270-86. Claims that San Juan's strophe is taken from Boscán's *coplas* VI and X.

LAPADAT, BASIL. "Diferencias técnicas entre Boscán y Garcilaso." *Acta Philologica,* III (1960), 203-20.

MARASSO, ARTURO. "Juan Boscán." *Estudios de literatura castellana.* Buenos Aires: Editorial Kapelusz, 1955. Pp. 1-34.

MENENDEZ PELAYO, MARCELINO. *Antología de poetas líricos castellanos: Boscán. Obras completas.* Santander: CSIC, 1945. Vol. XXVI (Vol. X of the *Antología*). First and only complete study of Boscán's life and works. Has four chapters which trace Boscán's life, the hendecasyllable before and in Boscán's verses, a "critical" analysis of Boscán's poetry, and the poet's posthumous fame.

MOGLIA, RAUL. "Manrique en un soneto de Boscán." *Revista de Filología Hispánica,* VIII (1945), 392-93. Boscán's "Quien dice que la ausencia causa olvido" (Sonnet LI) is inspired by Manrique's "Quien no estuviera en presencia."

MOLINARO, JULIUS A. "Boscán's Translation of *Il cortegiano* and his Linguistic Devices." *Quaderni Ibero-Americani,* No. 24 (1959), 584-93. The techniques Boscán used are: synonyms for variety, adding explanatory phrases to a certain word, elaborating or embellishing the text to make certain the meaning is clear, suppressing what he feels is already understood, condensing verbose passages, preferring more simple Spanish words to a more elegant one in the Italian, avoiding specialized or technical words, treating anecdotes with a certain freedom, and various minor syntactical changes.

MORREALE DE CASTRO, MARGHERITA. *Castiglione y Boscán: El ideal cortesano en el renacimiento español (Estudio léxico-semántico).* Madrid: Anejos del Boletín de la Real Academia Española 1, 1959. 2 vols. Volume I contains the studies "Boscán como traductor," "Algunas características de la versión del léxico," "Algunas acepciones de 'extraño' y su calor ponderativo," and all the other earlier published studies of Morreale on the topic. Volume II is a comparative vocabulary of the major lexicon in Castiglione's opus and Boscán's translation, plus a number of other linguistic appendixes.

_____. "'Claros y frescos ríos:' Imitación de Petrarca y reminiscencias de Castiglione en la segunda canción de Boscán." *Thesaurus,* VIII

(1952), 165–73. Shows the influence of Petrarch and Castiglione on Boscán's poetry.

_____. "'Cortegiano faceto,' y 'burlas cortesanas.'" *Boletín de la Real Academia Española,* XXXV (1955), 57–83. Examines the expressions used by Castiglione and Boscán for the analysis and description of laughter.

_____. "'Desenvoltura,' 'suelto' y 'soltura' en Boscán." *Revista de Filología Española,* XXXVIII (1954), 257–64. Studies the use of these words by Boscán in *El cortesano.*

_____. "El mundo del cortesano." *Revista de Filologia Española,* XLII (1958–59), 229–60. Studies the word "cortesano" as used before and by Castiglione and Boscán.

_____. "El superlativo en 'issimo' y la versión castellana del *Cortesano.*" *Revista de Filología Española,* XXXIX (1955), 46–60.

Osuna, R. "Unas coplas de Boscán publicadas en su vida." *Hispanic Review,* XXXI (1963), 103–8. Publishes an early version of "Tristeza pues soy tuyo" (*Copla* VII), printed in the *Cancionero de Juan de Molina* (1528).

Parducci, A. "Saggio sulla lirica di Juan Boscán." *Memorie della Accademia delle Scienze di Bologna,* III (1952), Series V.

Peers, E. Allison. "The Alleged Debts of San Juan de la Cruz to Boscán and Garcilaso de la Vega." *Hispanic Review,* XXI (1953), 1–19 and 93–106. The *lira* form of San Juan's "Llama de amor viva" comes from the *Boscán a lo divino* of Sebastián de Córdoba (Zaragoza, 1577). Peers lists all the alleged influences of Boscán on San Juan and finds most of them untenable.

_____. "New Interpretations of Spanish Poetry: VI — Two Sonnets by Boscán." *Bulletin of Spanish Studies,* XX (1946), 153–55. Translations and commentaries for "O gran fuerza de amor, que así enflaqueces" (LXIV) and "Soy como aquel que vive en el desierto" (LXXIV).

Percopo, Erasmo. "Giovanni Boscán e Luigi Tansillo." *Rassegna Critica della Letteratura Italiana,* XVII (1912), 193–210. Tansillo wrote six sonnets that express his admiration for the amorous verses of Boscán. All were written before 1543, which demonstrates the popularity of Boscán's poetry before official publication.

Peres, Ramon D. "El caso de Boscán." *Revue Hispanique,* LXXXI (1933), 475–89. Weak review of past studies on Juan Boscán.

Porter, Thaddeus C. *The Italianate Poetry of Juan Boscán.* Diss. Vanderbilt University, 1968. Summary study of Boscán's Italianate poetry. The thesis is most noteworthy for the sections comparing Boscán's verses with the sources in Petrarch and Bembo.

Reichenberger, Arnold G. "Boscán and the Classics." *Comparative Literature,* III (1951), 97–118. Comprehensive examination of

Boscán's borrowings from the Classics, especially that the opening poem to the Duchess of Somma imitates Catullus's introductory poem, and that "Leandro y Hero" comes from Musaeus, Ovid, and Virgil.

_____. "Boscán and Ovid." *Modern Language Notes,* LXV (1950), 379–83. Shows that Boscán's "Leandro y Hero" borrows heavily from Ovid's *Heroides* XVIII and XIX, and also somewhat from the *Metamorphoses.*

_____. "Boscán's *Epístola a Mendoza.*" *Hispanic Review,* XVII (1949), 1–17. Excellent analysis of Boscán's poetic letter to Diego Hurtado de Mendoza.

_____. "An Emendation of the Text of Boscán's *Historia de Leandro y Hero.*" *Modern Language Notes,* LXV (1950), 493. Changes the verse "las ninfas le *vencieron* y Nereo" to read "las ninfas le veneran a Nereo" because of *veneramur* in the source (Virgil's *Georgics* IV).

REIG, CAROLA. "Doña Ana Girón de Rebolledo, musa y editora de Boscán." *Escorial,* XV (1944), 289–302.

RIVERS, ELIAS L. "Garcilaso divorciado de Boscán." *Homenaje a Rodríguez Moñino,* II, 121–29. Madrid: Castalia, 1966. Points out that after the publication of Garcilaso's verse apart from Boscán's in 1569 only five more printings of the original volume with Boscán and Garcilaso together appeared.

_____. "The Horatian Epistle and Its Introduction into Spanish Literature." *Hispanic Review,* XXII (1954), 175–94. Compares Boscán's "Epistle to Mendoza" to Garcilaso's "Epistle to Boscán" and Mendoza's "Epistle to Boscán." Boscán's is the least Horatian because it stresses Christian themes, heterosexual love, a personal plan for life, and marriage.

SAROLLA, GIAN ROBERTO. "Boscán as Translator: St. Jerome or the Humanists?" *Modern Language Notes,* LXXVII (1962), 187–91. Boscán culled his ideas on translations from contemporary humanists.

SIMON DIAZ, JOSE. "Juan Boscán." *Bibliografía de la literatura hispánica,* VI, 622–34. Madrid: CSIC, 1973. Complete bibliography of all codices and editions of Boscán's works as well as most studies on the poet.

TREND, J. B. "Musical Settings of Famous Poets." *Revue Hispanique,* LXXI (1927), 547. Found the following pieces of Boscán's poetry set to music in sixteenth-century songbooks: "Claros y frescos ríos" (*Cancion* II), "El que sin ti vivir" ("Epístola"), "Mi corazón fatigado" (*Copla* VI), and "Si no es hubiera mirado" (*Villancico* I).

Appendices

A. Boscán's manifesto on the adoption of the Italianate meters:
"To the Duchess of Somma"

I fear I am pestering your majesty with so many Books. But now that
the importunity can't be excused, I consider it probably not as bad as
giving the volume to you separated in Parts; because if the first Book
should bore you, an easy remedy is to set aside the others. Although it now
occurs to me that the fourth Book is going to be Garcilaso's *Works;* and I
hope that section will not only not bore anyone, but rather will alleviate
the boredom caused by the others. In the first Book your majesty has seen
those *coplas* (I want to refer to them that way) written in the Castilian
style. Diego de Mendoza, a very well-informed man whom you know quite
well, used to entertain himself with them. But I think that he amused himself as with children, and therefore he called them *redondillas*. This second
Book will have different verses, written in the Italian style, which will be
sonnets and *canciones;* for the metrical compositions of this art have
always been called by these names. Their manner is graver and of more
artistry, and, if I am not mistaken, much better than the manner of the
Castilian poetry. But still, notwithstanding, when I decided to try them
out, I assumed that I would have many detractors in the matter. Because
the form was new in our country, and the writers new also, at least most of
them; and with so much novelty it was impossible not to fear with just
cause, and even without it. All the more, as soon as I set to work I met men
who utterly bored me, and in a matter in which everything consists in
ingenuity and wit, these two things not having any more life than they have
of pleasure, since it bored me it also had to disgust me, and after being
disgusted, I had nowhere else to go. Some complained that in the metrical
composition of this art the consonants did not fit so closely nor sound so
well as in the Castilian verses. Others said that they were not sure if this
verse was verse or if it was prose. Others argued that the verses had to be
principally for women, and that they did not treat weighty matters but
only the sounds of the words and the sweetness of the consonantal rhyme.
   These men's opinions moved me to try to understand the matter better,
because by understanding it I would see their unjust statements more
clearly. And thus the more I have tried to terminate the matter discussing it

133

with myself and speaking of it with others, the more I have seen what little basis they have to instill these reservations in me; and their arguments have seemed so unjustified that I get angry for ever having thought about them at all, and I would get angrier now if I should have to respond to their complaints. For, who ought to respond to men who are moved only by the sound of the consonantal rhyme? And, who ought to argue with people who do not know what a verse is unless it is shod and saddled with consonantal rhyme, entering all of a sudden through one ear and coming out the other? As for the others who say that these poems are not very weighty because they are only for women, who is going to waste time responding to them? I consider women of such substance, those who succeed in being so, and many do succeed, that whoever should try to defend them in this matter would offend them. So for these men, and all those of their ilk, they have permission to say what they wish, because I do not plan on being very friendly with them; for if they should speak badly of me, I would have to speak well in order to cut them off. If my poetry appears to them to be hard sounding, and if they should want the company of a multitude of consonantal rhyme, there is their Songbook, which is called the *Cancionero general,* so that everybody in general can be entertained by it. And if they want jokes, they will also find them at little cost.

What now remains for me to inform those who should read this Book is that they should not take me for such a friend of new things that they should consider the only reason I wanted to try out these rhymes was to make myself the inventor of them, which until now we had not seen in Spain. On the contrary, I want them to know that I never made a profession out of writing this, nor any other thing; nor, even if I could, would I set to work testing other new inventions. I know very well how great the danger is in writing, and I understand that many of those who have written, even though they have done it more than passingly well, if they are wise, ought to have repented innumerable times. So if I have also been afraid of writing, no matter how easy it should be for me, I would be much more afraid to try out my pen on what until now no one else in our Spain had attempted. Thus if I write after all this, and I have what I wrote printed, and I have decided to be the first that has joined the Castilian tongue with the Italian way of writing, it appears that such a decision contradicts what I say with what I do. To this I answer that as for the writing I now gave enough reason in the Prologue of the first Book. As for trying the style of these sonnets and *canciones,* and other forms in this genre, I respond that in all that I have written I never wrote professionally, but just to entertain my spirits, if I have any, and this to spend less worriedly some of the worrisome moments in life, so also in this case of invention (if they want to call it thus), I never thought that I would invent nor make anything that would endure in the world, but I began it carelessly, as with something that required so little to do it, that there was no reason not to do it, having the desire to do it. What is more, it came up during a conversation. Because one day when in Granada with Navaggiero (whom I have wanted to mention by name to your majesty because he was such a celebrated figure of our time) talking with him about matters of ingenuity and letters, and especially about the variety of many languages, he asked me why I did not try to write in the Castilian tongue some sonnets and other art forms used by the good authors of Italy; and he not only asked me directly in that way, but he even begged me to do it. I left for home a few days later, and with the length and loneliness of the trip I thought about diverse things, and I was brought back many times to what Navaggiero had said to me; and thus I began to try out this poetic genre. At the beginning I found some difficulty with it, because it was so artistic and had so many different peculiarities from our own. But finding afterwards, perhaps out of egotism, that I was having some success with it, I began little by little to take the project seriously. But this would not have been enough to make me go on if Garcilaso with his sound judgment — which, not only in my opinion but in everybody's, has been taken for granted by everyone — had not hardened my resolve in the enterprise. And thus often praising my project and terminating by approving it with his own examples, because he also wished to travel this road, he finally made me spend all my free hours only on this matter. And after I had cleared my mind with all his persuasion, more reasons came to me each day to continue the work already begun. I realized that this verse the Castilians use, if we look at it closely, has totally unknown origins. And if it were so good that it could be approved of on its own merits, as the other verses which are good, there would be no need to scrutinize who were its inventors; because it would establish its authority by itself, and it would not be necessary to give it authority on account of those who invented it. But now it does not bring anything to itself by which it should receive more honor than it does, which is to be accepted by the masses, nor does it show us its origins with the authority of which we would be obligated to honor it. All this is exactly the opposite from this verse in our second Book. Because in it we see wherever we look a very capable disposition to receive any kind of material, whether solemn or subtle or difficult or easy; and likewise in order to join with any other style of those that we find among the approved ancient authors. More than this, it has left such good evidence of its worthiness wherever it has passed that if we wish to take it from here where it has reached us and return with it back along the road from which it came, we can very easily approach its origin. And thus we see it now in our days be well-treated in Italy, which is a land flowering with geniuses in rhetoric, wit, and literature.

Petrarch was the first one in that country to perfect it, and it has remained and will remain in that perfection. Dante was earlier; he used it very well, but in a different way than Petrarch. In Dante's time and a little earlier the Provençal poets flourished, whose works, because of the times, are virtually unknown. Among these Provençal poets were many excellent Catalan writers. The best of them is Ausias March, in whose praise, if I should begin, I would not return so quickly to what I am now discussing. But the testimony of Admiral Fadrique Enríquez is sufficient, for after he saw his works for the first time, he had them copied with much care and is as acquainted with the verses as well as, as they say, Alexander was with Homer's poetry. But to return to our topic, I say that even going further back than the Provençal poets, we will find still the road made by our verse. Because the hendecasyllables, about which the Latins have made such ado, carry almost the same style, and are indeed the same as much as the difference in language allows. And we have not yet reached the source, for the Latins were not the inventors either, but took it from the Greeks, as they have taken many other things in diverse fields. So this poetic genre, both with the authority of its own value and with the reputation of the ancients and moderns who have used it, is worthy not only of being received by a language so good as Castilian, but even of being preferred in that language over all the popular verses. And thus I think that it is on the way to becoming so preferred; because now the good intellectuals of Castile that work outside of the popular vein love it and follow it, and use it so much, that if the times with their upheavels do not destroy it, before long the Italians will be complaining that their poetry was transferred to Spain all too well. But that time is still far off, and it is not good that we found our hopes until we see them closer. What the present writers can be proud of is that they should have a judge of such authority as Your Magesty, because the good poets are favored and the bad ones undeceived. But it is now time for the second Book to speak for itself, and to show how it goes with its sonnets and *canciones;* and if things should not turn out as well as one should desire, remember that the first artists do enough just by beginning, and it remains for the others who come afterwards to better it.

B. Cristóbal de Castillijo's opposition to the Italianate meters: "Censure of Spanish Poets Who Write with Italian Meters"

Since the Holy Inquisition is accustomed to be so diligent in justifiably punishing any newly formed sect and opinion, let Lucero return from the dead to correct one in Spain as strange and new as Luther's in Germany.

They can rightly be punished as if they were Anabaptists, since they are getting rebaptized according to their own laws, and they call themselves Petrarchists. They have rejected the Faith in Castilian meters, and they lose their souls seeking after the Italian ones, saying that these are richer and more lyrical.

I leave the judgment of all this with those who know best; but it is not befitting that anyone judge his natural fatherland to be lacking in elegance. The Christian muse of the famous Juan de Mena, feeling great sorrow about this, accuses them of being infidels and condemns them for being traitors.

"Let the sleeping soul awake," proclaims Jorge de Montemayor; and shows his sorrow at such a daring thing, for no more can be said. Garci-Sánchez responded: "Who would grant me, my lady, life and wisdom at this hour to go out on the battlefield against such a sinful people?"

"If there be a God of love," Cartegena then said, "let him show his valor here against such great audacity, imported from a foreign land." Torres Naharro replies: "You consent to such malevolences, Love, only to show your deeds, and so that our rich Spain will be deprived of its rights."

May God give his glory to Boscán and to the poet Garcilaso, who with no little eagerness sustained this sect, and left it now disseminated among the people; for which justly happened to them what this following sonnet describes:

Sonnet

Garcilaso and Boscán, having come to the place where were
the troubadours who were so dextrous in our tongue and its
niceties, found them glancing one at the others with pale
faces, fearing the two were spies or lawless enemies;
for, judging first by their clothes, the two seemed to
them to be, as they should be, genteel Spanish knights,
but hearing the two speak the new language mixed with foreign
poetry, they looked on the two men as strangers.

But these two men, even though they were so out of favor and alone, stood up against everybody and openly scoffed at the Spanish *coplas, canciones,* and *villancicos, romances* and such, *arte mayor* and *arte real,* and *pies quebrados* and *pies chicos,* and all our cache.

And in place of these vowel-forms now well known in our homespun meters, they sing other foreign ones, new to our ears: sonnets of great esteem, madrigals and *canciones* of different lines, with octaves and *terza rima* and other new inventions.

They despise anything composed before with *coplas* as base and vile. They use instead a type of measured prose without consonantal rhyme. They consider many of the old forms that were elegant and discreet as simple and poor children solely because they did not fit into the sonnet count.

Finally, they declared that those old authors did not know how to make good meters nor to write stylistically about love; and they said that the Castilian meter did not have the authority to say majestically what is said with better results in Tuscan.

But they do not attribute this fault or lack to our tongue, which is true enough, but they say that it was only the absence of good writers; and they accredit this absence to the fact that in the past all lacked these excellent meters that the present moderns have discovered and found.

Seeing thus how they presumed about their new science, the troubadours told the two that they wanted to see something of what they wrote; for proof of which, as an example of the new use, each one composed a *rima* for the occasion, which is published here below.

Sonnet

If the pains you instill are real, as my soul knows all
too well, why do they not kill me? and death without them
would be even more real. And if perhaps the pains are
illusory and want to frolic with my happiness, tell me:
why do they kill me each day with pain in a thousand different
ways? Show me this secret now, my lady; let me know from
you, if what I suffer is death or life; because, since you
are the murderer, I do not desire greater glory from my
pain than to be able to affirm such a homicide.

Octave

Now that my torments are forced upon me, it is for the
best that they are consented to without force. What
greater alleviation is there for my cares than to be suffering
because of you? If they are well employed in your service,
my lady, by being recognized by you, the greatest anguish
of my pain would be full of peace and glory.

When Juan de Mena heard the new meters he was content; in fact, he smiled as if he knew about them and said: "As for proof, I find no cause to consider new a line with eleven syllables, since I myself used them."

Don Jorge said: "I do not see any need or reason to dress up with new desire *coplas* that go in circles to state their intention. Our language is very devoted to clear brevity, and this meter, in truth, denotes on the contrary obscure prolixity."

Garci-Sánchez showed himself to be quite angry, and said: "It is not fair to claim that what was born in Spain comes from a foreign land; because in my *Liciones* alone, if one looks well at its strophes, you will see such consonantal rhyme that Petrarch and his *canciones* are left behind in elegance."

Cartagena, being an expert in love matters, then said: "With the strength of this fire these new troubadours will not win the game from us;

these verses, in my opinion, are very melancholic and difficult to read, slow in plot and enemies of pleasure."

Torres said: "If I had thought that the Castilian tongue would suffer sonnets composed by me, I could easily have done them, since I wrote them in Latin; but I take no joy in such haughty verses, always written so honestly that they run with leaden feet and are heavy-hipped."

Finally, the conclusion was reached that out of courtesy and for the sake of honoring the invention on the nation's part, they would declare the verses worthy of praise. And in order that all could manifest this favor, a troubadour here below was charged with writing a sonnet in their praise.

Sonnet

Italian and Latin muses, people from such foreign parts,
such new and beautiful carnations, how have you gotten to
our Spain? Who brought you to be neighbors of the Tajo, of
its mountains and fields? Or who is he who guides and
accompanies you through such strange lands of pilgrimage?
— Don Diego de Mendoza and Garcilaso brought us, and Boscán
and Luis de Haro by order and protection of the god Apollo.
Death carried two of them slowly by, Suleiman another, and
only don Diego remains to succor us, but he alone is enough.

C. "Boscán's Conversion"

1. Después que por este suelo
   mil engaños descubrí,
   un poco tornando en mí,
   sin osar mirar al cielo,
   preguntéme: qué es de tí?
   Los ojos alcé por verme,
   y en verme ví tan mortal
   que pues no puedo valerme,
   por no conocerme tal,
   no quisiera conocerme.

   After I discovered on this earth
   a thousand deceits,
   having returned a little to myself,
   without daring to look at heaven,
   I asked myself: What about you?
   I raised by eyes to see myself,
   and on seeing me I saw such mortality
   that since I cannot take care of myself,
   in order not to know myself in such a state,
   I would not wish to know myself.

2. Conocí la enfermedad
   de mi mal conocimiento,
   ví confuso al pensamiento,
   y suelta la voluntad,
   y atado el entendimiento.
   Ví mi alma como va
   muerta con su misma guerra,

   I recognized my sickness to be
   a lack of self-recognition;
   I saw the thinking faculties confused,
   the will turned loose,
   and the understanding bound.
   I saw how my soul is
   dead with its self-inflicted war,

y víla enterrada ya,
puesta debaxo de tierra,
pues debaxo el cuerpo está.

and I saw it buried already,
deposited beneath the earth,
since it is beneath the body.

3. Ví mi seso como es,
que a cada paso estropieza;
víme tornado al revés,
los pies sobre la cabeza,
la cabeza so los pies.
El orden ví natural,
en mí todo trastornado:
porque ví sojuzgado
lo inmortal a lo mortal,
y lo flaco a lo esforzado.

I saw how my rational faculties are,
for they stumble with each step;
I saw myself turned upside-down,
the feet above my head,
the head under my feet.
I saw the natural order of things
all reversed in me
because I saw subjected
the immortal to the mortal,
and the weak to the strong.

4. Ví la parte que se muestra
por muestra de Dios en todos,
a la parte más siniestra,
derribada de sus modos,
atinada de mal diestra.
Lo malo se encarecía,
lo bueno daba de balde,
no sé quién ví que ponía
al deseo por alcalde,
por reyna a la fantasía.

I saw the part that shows itself
as the imprint of God in all beings,
in the most wretched part,
torn down by its habits,
hit upon the wrong mark.
The bad was prized,
the good was freely given away,
I saw I know not who that put
Desire as the mayor,
Fantasy as the queen.

5. Vi mis quatro calidades,
que de fuerza son contrarias,
convertidas de adversarias
para todas mis maldades.
Conformes y voluntarias,
consintiendo en lo peor,
a tener paz fui venido,
mas debiera yo perdido
ganalla por vencedor,
y ganéla por vencido.

I saw my four elements,
which by nature are contrary,
converted into adversaries
by all my iniquities.
In agreement and voluntary,
consenting to what was worse,
I was resolved to have peace,
but I ought to have lost
winning it as a victor,
and I won it by defeat.

6. Ya llegaba a estar contento,
en disformidad conforme,
satisfecho el pensamiento
de que ví que era disforme
la casa con el cimiento.
Holgaba de estar confuso,
huía de qualquier cura,

I even became content,
in a conforming nonconformity,
the thinking faculties satisfied
with the fact that I saw the house
to be wrong for its foundation.
I took pleasure in being confused,
I fled from any kind of cure,

y en esta mi compostura
gobernaba el solo uso,
y cesaba la natura.

and in this kind of composure
habit alone governed,
and the natural instincts ceased.

7. Como doliente dañado
de dañada fantasía,
que aborrece lo poblado,
y en mitad quiere del día
de la luz estar privado;
yo así donde el bien moraba,
y alumbraba la razón,
tan presto me fatigaba,
que en el mal del corazón
solamente reposaba.

As a patient wounded
by a wounded fantasy,
that abhors populace places,
and in the middle of the day desires
to be deprived of sunlight;
I thus where good lived,
and reason illuminated,
became so quickly fatigued
that only in the illness of my heart
did I find repose.

8. En el más baxo elemento
era mi placer y gloria;
allí estaba el pensamiento
preparando en la memoria
deleytes al sentimiento.
Arrastrado por el suelo
mi juicio tanto yerra,
que tuviera por consuelo,
si quien hizo mar y tierra
se olvidara hacer el cielo.

In the lowest element
was my pleasure and glory;
there were my thinking faculties
preparing in the memory
delights for the feelings.
Dragged along the ground
my judgment errs so much
that I would have it for consolation
if He who made the sea and earth
would have forgotten to make heaven.

9. Con ceguedad muy estraña,
tan contraria de mi nombre,
aunque todo el mal me engaña,
con la parte que fui hombre
conocí ser alimaña.
Aquel ser con que nací
tan del todo se perdió,
que entonces en mí se vió
ninguna cosa de mí
tan lexos como fui yo.

With a very strange blindness,
so contrary to my good name,
although the illness deceives me,
with the part of me that was human
I recognized to be animalistic.
That being with which I was born
was lost so entirely,
that then I saw in myself
nothing that was me,
so far from myself was I.

10. Aunque al mal yo no repuno,
estando un poco despierto
víme dos hombres en uno;
y al cabo fue lo más cierto,
que ví que no fue ninguno.
De mí mismo gana hube
entonces, de me probar,

Although I do not repulse the illness,
being a little awake
I saw myself as two men in one;
and finally the most certain was
that I saw I was neither one nor the other.
By my own decision I desired
then to test myself,

mas de vergüenza que tuve,   but I was ashamed;
no siendo para reynar,   not being able to reign,
en mi reyno me detuve.   I remained in my realm.

11. Puesto que era tan perdido,   Since I was so lost,
    del mal pensé apartarme;   I considered departing from the illness;
    mas quando quise mudarme,   but when I wished to move,
    según estaba tollido,   since I was so crippled,
    no fue posible mudarme.   it was not possible to move.
    Dióme luego tal tristeza,   This gave me such sad feelings,
    viendo el mal que así se esfuerza, seeing how the illness thus gained strength,
    que, según fue su grandeza,   that, since its greatness was such,
    queriendo probar mi fuerza,   wishing to prove my own strength,
    fue probada mi flaqueza.   my weakness was proven.

12. Socorro no me faltaba,   Aid was not lacking,
    solevantarme quería;   and wanted to raise me up;
    mas aquel que me ayudaba,   but that person who was helping me,
    al principio socorría,   at the beginning aided,
    y en el medio me dexaba.   and in the middle left me.
    No dexaba su tristeza   His sadness at aiding me
    jamás de mi socorrer;   never left;
    pero ni dió su poder   but neither did he give his strength
    con lo que por mi flaqueza   with which my weakness
    se pudiera sostener.   could be sustained.

13. Como niño que no anda,   As a child who does not walk,
    mas anda por andar ya,   but who walks because he is of age to do it,
    que si es cuerdo el que lo manda the person who orders it is wise
    do quiera que con él va,   enough to go with him and
    poco a poco se desmanda;   requires it little by little;
    así aquel que me llevaba,   thus that person who carried me,
    como a niño me traía,   brought me as a child.
    los principios me mostraba,   He showed me the first steps,
    lo demás que no cabía,   the rest that did not fit,
    do cabía lo guardaba.   he waited until it would fit.

14. Yo llegaba al primer grado   I reached the first level
    de la gracia que se empieza,   of beginning grace,
    donde aquel que es ya llegado,   where the person who has already arrived,
    si no pierde la cabeza,   if he does not lose his head,
    se tiene por librado.   considers himself well freed.
    Ya la luz esclarecía,   Now the light began to clear,
    la tiniebla se quebraba,   the darkness was breaking up,

aunque el sol no parecía do el cielo no se cerraba, se mostraba el claro día.	although the sun did not appear. Where the sky was not overcast the clear day showed through.

15. Yo viendo que amaneciera,
comencé de apercebirme;
Ya era tiempo de partirme,
pero no de tal manera
que pudiese bien regirme.
Poco a poco recordaba,
porque estaba tan pesado,
que el sueño que me quedaba
del sueño que era pasado,
parece que me turbaba.

I, seeing that it was dawning,
began to prepare myself;
now was the time to depart,
but not in such a way
that I could control myself well.
Little by little I began to remember;
but it was quite difficult,
because the sleepiness that remained
from the sleep that was past
seemed to disturb me.

16. Como pastor que ha dormido
en la noche en su cabaña,
que viniendo la mañana
se levanta amodorrido,
y se va por la montaña,
y soplándose las manos
se sacude y se despierta;
así el alma que era muerta
en deseos harto vanos,
se halló que fue despierta.

As a shepherd who has slept
in his cabin all night,
seeing the morning,
rises up heavy with sleep
and goes along the mountain
and blowing on his hands
shakes himself and wakes up,
thus my soul which was dead
in too vain desires
found itself awake.

17. Del cielo hasta el abismo
ví el ayre quasi sereno,
y acordando mi baptismo,
conocí que tan ageno
fuera siempre de mí mismo;
y ví el sol en su semblante
tan hermoso y tan luciente,
que aunque estaba en el oriente,
tanta luz en un instante
se mostraba en el poniente,

From heaven to the abyss
I saw the air almost serene,
and, remembering my baptism,
I recognized that I had been
always so foreign to myself;
and I saw the sun in its countenance
so beautiful and splendid
that although it was in the east,
it gave so much light that immediately
it illuminated the west.

18. El socorro ya segundo
comenzaba a socorrerme,
con el qual pude valerme
de los males deste mundo,
sin peligro de perderme.
De mi mal quedaba sano,

A second aid now
began to aid me,
with which I could seek help
from the illnesses of this world,
without danger of losing me.
I remained cured of my illness

pero no tan sin trabajo
que fuese tan en mi mano
caminar por el atajo
como pude por lo llano.

19. Del sueño muy recordado,
tirando para la cumbre
me hallé tan levantado
que en mí solo la costumbre
me quedaba del pecado.
A la culpa me tornaba
el huir del alma mía,
el mal yo le concebía;
mas tan presto le mataba
que luego le malparía.

20. Entonces de nuevo hecho
ví el ser de mi corazón,
que se viera tan deshecho
que en el alma la razón
era todo su despecho.
Criado como de nada
ví mi hombre que está dentro,
tan rehecho allá en su centro,
que la vida dél pasada
la llevaba de un encuentro.

21. Dexando de ser ageno,
fui hecho como en un punto,
a fin que todo muy junto
sobre aquello que es más bueno
yo llevase el contrapunto;
porque aquel que me crió,
que en todo se satisfizo,
muchas veces me formó:
la primera vez me hizo,
las otras me convirtió.

22. De ser tan alto subido,
como digo, y trasformado,
en mi orden ordenado,
ví mi reyno muy regido
por razón y no por grado.

but not without so much work
that it was in my hands
to walk along the rocky path
as well as I could on the plain.

Well awakened from my sleep,
headed for the summit,
I found myself so enlightened
that only the habit of sinning
remained with me.
The blame tried to return to me
as my soul fled.
I conceived now the illness
but I killed it so quickly
that it immediately miscarried.

Then I saw made anew
the being of my heart,
which was so undone
that in the soul reason
was its total despair.
Created as if from nothing,
I saw the human part that is inside
so remade there in the center
that the past life
was carried away in the encounter.

Ceasing to be foreign to myself,
I was made now of one piece,
to the end that all together
over that which is the best
I carried the counterpoint;
because the person Who created me,
Who satisfied Himself with all,
many times formed me:
the first time He made me,
the other times He converted me.

From being raised up so high
as I say, and transformed,
ordered to my order,
I saw my kingdom ruled well
by reason and not by pleasure.

Mis tres almas a la par
ví puestas en exercicio,
cada una en su oficio:
la una para mandar,
y las dos para servicio.

23. Ví luego la fantasía
como mozo rezongando;
mas razón no permitía,
por el bien del otro bando,
que pasase su porfía.
Ví mis torpes sentimientos,
aunque no quisiera vellos,
y hallé según sus tientos
que sólo quedaba dellos
los primeros movimientos.

24. Y ví la más alta esfera
del alma que gobernaba;
y según me pareciera,
por de dentro calentaba,
y alumbraba por de fuera.
Allí ví el entendimiento
con la verdad por objeto,
y ví todo el regimiento
tan cerca de ser perfeto,
que me hizo estar contento.

25. Ví la voluntad con mando
absoluto y ordinario,
que por mejorar su bando,
hasta el bien extraordinario
se iba de quando en quando.
Ví la parte que es espuela
para la salud, y freno;
ví amor que puso vela
del deseo que de bueno
va pagado con la tela.

26. Ví más el alta memoria,
tesoro de bien humano,
donde ví larga la historia
de mi ser que fue tan vano,

I saw my three souls
working together,
each one doing his office,
one commanding
and the other two serving.

I then saw my fantasy
as a grumbling child;
but reason did not permit
for the good of the other faction
that its persistence should continue.
I saw my stupefied sentiments,
although I did not wish to see them,
and I found, according to their temptations,
that only remained
their first movements.

I saw the highest sphere
of the soul governing,
and it appeared to me
that it was creating heat
and illuminating what was outside.
There I saw the understanding
as the object of truth,
and I saw all the regiment
so close to being perfect
that I became content.

I saw the will
in absolute and regular command,
who, in order to better its team,
went from time to time
toward the extraordinary good.
I saw the part that is the spur
for health, and the brake;
I saw that love, who set sail
from desire, went
with the sail well trimmed.

Moreover, I saw lofty memory,
treasure of human well-being,
where I saw the long history
of my life that was so vain,

que no fue para dar gloria.
Fue bien haberme acordado
de mi triste mal ausente,
pues mi alma ya consiente
que acordando lo pasado
se corrija lo presente.

27. Lo pasado y por venir,
todo lo puso delante,
y de haber sido inconstante
me vino ella a repetir,
que me hizo ser constante.
Trastornaba mi conciencia
lo que es, y lo que era,
todo puesto en mi presencia,
de mí que el mando tuviera
se tomaba residencia.

28. Dolor de la culpa mía
de la culpa me libraba,
porque así me castigaba
que solo pesar tenía,
si pesar no me sobraba.
Mereciendo en el holgar
que hube del padecer
tan presto estaba en llorar
que mil veces mi placer
renovaba mi penar.

29. Por crecer en el dolor
de mi pasada locura,
contemplando el Hacedor
me acordé de la hechura
de mí, triste pecador.
Ví que Dios me redimió
contra sí siendo cruel,
y mirando bien lo dél
ví como se hizo él yo,
porque yo me hiciese él.

30. Ví que quando me formara,
ningún estado me diera,
mas en mi mano pusiera
que yo mismo me tomara

that was not for gaining glory.
It was good to have remembered,
absent from my sad illness,
since my soul now agrees
that by remembering what is past
what is present can be corrected.

It put present all
that was past and future
and, for having been inconstant,
it came to repeat to me
that which made me be constant.
My conscience upturned
what is and what was,
all placed in my presence;
it took up residence in me
that I should take control.

Pain of my faults
freed me from the faults
because thus was castigated
who only felt sorrow,
if sorrow was not too much for me.
Meriting in the restfulness
that I had from suffering
so quickly was I in crying
that a thousand times my pleasure
renewed my pain.

By increasing the pain
of my past madness,
contemplating the Maker,
I remembered my creatureliness,
a sad sinner.
I saw that God redeemed me
by being cruel to Himself;
and by looking well at His example
I saw how He acted,
so I could act like Him.

I saw that when He formed me
He gave me no state,
but He put in my hand
that I myself should take

aquello que más quisiera;
que pudiese ser bestial,
o pudiese ser humano,
o que fuese angelical,
o que estuviese en mi mano
de tomar lo divinal.

that which I should desire;
that I could be bestial
or I could be human
or I could be angelical,
or that it was in my hand
to take what was divine.

31. Ví su alta providencia
    do lo por hacer es hecho,
    que jamás me dió sentencia
    que no fuese por provecho
    de mi sola conociencia.
    Ví la causa por que quiso
    haber hecho fuego eterno,
    y fue para darme aviso
    por guardarme del infierno
    que ganase el paraíso.

    I saw His great providence,
    where what is future is present,
    that He never gave me advice
    that was not to the advantage
    of my own self-knowledge.
    I saw why He desired
    to have made eternal fire;
    and it was in order to warn me,
    to protect me from hell
    that I should gain paradise.

32. Ví que quando me justicia
    va forzado y con discordia,
    que a poder de mi malicia
    queriendo misericordia
    le hago querer justicia.
    Viendo esto ví tal vena
    en mí de arrepentimiento
    que bastó para descuento
    un momento desta pena
    para el eternal tormento.

    I saw that when He judges me,
    it goes forced and with discord,
    that in spite of my malice,
    desiring mercy,
    I make Him desire justice.
    Seeing this, I saw such a vein
    of repentance in me
    that it was enough to discount
    a moment of this pain
    for eternal torment.

33. Fue tan alto convertirme,
    y de Dios tan ayudado,
    que luego al muy alto grado,
    con mi propósito firme,
    me ví que fui sublimado.
    Tan dentro me vi a la puerta,
    tan en paz y tan arriba,
    la guerra tan lexos iba,
    que la carne estuvo muerta
    de quedar el alma viva.

    So great was the desire to convert myself,
    and I was so aided by God,
    that immediately to the very highest level,
    with my firm proposal,
    I saw that I was sublimated.
    I saw the gateway so deep within me,
    so much at peace and so high,
    the war was so far away,
    that the flesh was dead
    because the soul was now alive.

34. De las gracias la postrera,
    aquella que nos confirma,
    tras la segunda y primera,

    With the final grace,
    that one that confirms us
    after the first and second,

poniendo luego su firma,
dexóme desta manera;
dexóme con tal salud
y en tal estado me puso,
que de dentro en mí compuso
con natura la virtud,
y con la virtud el uso.

35. Como ciego en quien se ofrece
tener la calidad tal,
y que así se compadece,
y su ser de ser igual,
ni se altera, ni adolece;
así el alma en sustancia
sus calidades ponía,
con tan igual consonancia,
que en ella ya no podía
tener poder inconstancia.

putting then His signature,
He left me in this state.
He left me with such health
and on such a plane He put me,
that He composed within me
virtue as second nature,
and with virtue, good habits.

As a blind man in whom is offered
to have such a quality
and who thus consoles himself
and his being with being equal
does not alter nor suffer,
thus the soul in substance
put its qualities
with such equal consonance
that it was not possible in it
to have any inconstancy.

Index

(The works of Boscán are listed under his name)

149